MODELING WITH AUTOCAD DESIGNER

The Irwin Graphics Series

Providing you with the highest quality textbooks that meet your changing needs requires feedback, improvement, and revision. The team of authors and Richard D. Irwin Publishers are committed to this effort. We invite you to become part of our team by offering your wishes, suggestions, and comments for future editions and new products and texts.

Please mail or fax your comments to: Sandra Dobek
Ryan Ranschaert
c/o Richard D. Irwin Publishers
1333 Burr Ridge Parkway
Burr Ridge, IL 60521
fax 708-789-6946

Titles in the Irwin Graphics Series include:

Engineering Graphics Communication by Bertoline, Wiebe, Miller, and Nasman, 1995

Technical Graphics Communication by Bertoline, Wiebe, Miller, and Nasman, 1995

Fundamentals of Graphics Communication by Bertoline, Wiebe, Miller, and Nasman, 1996

Problems for Engineering Graphics Communication and Technical Graphics Communication, Workbook #1, 1995.

Problems for Engineering Graphics Communication and Technical Graphics Communication, Workbook #2, 1995.

Problems for Engineering Graphics Communication and Technical Graphics Communication, Workbook #3, 1995.

AutoCAD Instructor Release 12 by James A. Leach, 1995

AutoCAD Companion Release 12 by James A. Leach, 1995

AutoCAD 13 Instructor by James A Leach, 1996

AutoCAD 13 Companion by James A Leach, 1996

CADKEY Companion by John Cherng, 1995

Hands-On CADKEY by Timothy Sexton, 1995

Engineering Design and Visualization Workbook by Dennis Stevenson, 1995

Modeling with AutoCAD Designer by Sandra Dobek and Ryan Ranschaert, 1996

MODELING WITH AutoCAD DESIGNER

Sandra Dobek

Ryan Ranschaert

IRWIN

Chicago • Bogotá • Boston • Buenos Aires • Caracas
London • Madrid • Mexico City • Sydney • Toronto

© Richard D. Irwin, a Times Mirror Higher Education Group, Inc. company, 1996

AutoCAD® Designer is a registered trademark of Autodesk, Inc. Passages on pages 38, 323, 375, and 376, are used courtesy of Autodesk, Inc. AutoCAD® Designer Dialogue Boxes, pulldown menus, and toolbar buttons are used with the permission from and under the copyright of Autodesk, Inc.

Irwin Book Team

Publisher: *Tom Casson*
Senior sponsoring editor: *Elizabeth A. Jones*
Editorial assistant: *Bradley Kosirog*
Senior marketing manager: *Brian Kibby*
Project editor: *Beth Cigler*
Production supervisor: *Pat Frederickson*
Designer: *Matthew Baldwin*
Compositor: *Precision Graphic Services Inc.*
Printer: *Malloy Lithographers*

Times Mirror
Higher Education Group

Libary of Congress Cataloging-in-Publication Data
Dobek, Sandra.
    Modeling for AutoCAD Designer / Sandra Dobek, Ryan Ranschaert.
        p.   cm.
    Includes index.
    ISBN 0-256-21376-3
    1. Computer graphics   2. AutoCAD Designer.   3. Computer-aided
design.   I. Ranschaert, Ryan.   II. Title.
T385.D63   1996
620'.0042'02855369—dc20   95–43381

Printed in the United States of America
1 2 3 4 5 6 7 8 9 0 ML 3 2 1 0 9 8 7 6

This book is dedicated to our family and friends for
their continuous support and understanding
throughout this project.

PREFACE

Welcome to *Modeling with AutoCAD® Designer*. It is our intention to teach you the fundamentals of AutoCAD Designer and the parametric modeling process. We believe that effective teaching of a graphics program takes more than just words and pictures. Students also need hands-on experience to learn how to use a three-dimensional modeling program. This book brings you a complete learning tool by effectively combining descriptive explanations and graphical illustrations with basic tutorials for nearly every AutoCAD Designer command.

The layout of this book is much like the program itself in that AutoCAD Designer's modeling process begins with a base feature that is expanded with additional features until the model is complete. *Modeling with AutoCAD Designer's* teaching process is much the same. After an overview of the entire modeling process, it begins with the basics of creating a solid part and then follows with various options and features. Questions and exercises at the end of each chapter ensure your full understanding of the material before you move ahead.

The book is based on AutoCAD Designer Release 1.2 and uses the standard typed characters for accessing all AutoCAD Designer commands. Windows® icons appear next to commands where applicable. In addition, a full listing of the AutoCAD Designer pull-down menus is provided at the back of the book.

We assume that the user of this book already has a basic understanding of AutoCAD; however, this background is not necessary. The appendix explains how to use the basic AutoCAD commands you need to get through AutoCAD Designer.

The goal of this book is to give you a full understanding of AutoCAD Designer and the parametric modeling process within a framework of some basic design and drafting principles. Although the book is geared toward the engineering and graphics students, the material is presented so that anyone who wants to learn about AutoCAD Designer and the parametric modeling process can do so. Parametric solid modeling is an exciting new technique to three-dimensional part creation. It is our intention to get you started on the creation of parametric models. Once you master the basic procedures, the possibilities are truly endless.

CONTENTS

1

MODELING WITH AUTOCAD® DESIGNER

AutoCAD® Designer is a parametric-based, three-dimensional modeling program. **Parameters** can be thought of in terms of dimensional variables, such as length, height, and width, or geometrical **constraints,** such as horizontal, vertical, and tangent. Models in AutoCAD Designer are made by relating features to one another parametrically. AutoCAD Designer allows you to create a feature-based model, and it also automatically updates the entire model when parameters are changed. A **feature** is a two-dimensional sketch that has been extruded, revolved, or swept along a path. **Holes, fillets,** and **chamfers** are also examples of features. All **models** in AutoCAD Designer are created in **Model space,** also referred to as **Part mode.** These terms are used interchangeably throughout the book.

This chapter walks you through the creation of a bookshelf, examines each step in the modeling process, and explains when and why certain commands are used. When complete, the final model will resemble Figure 1–1.

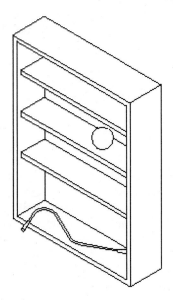

Figure 1–1

AutoCAD Designer's parametric process begins with the basic **sketch,** which does not need to be precise. Think of a sketch as a pencil drawing on paper made without a ruler. AutoCAD Designer interprets sketches according to a set of predetermined sketching rules; for example, a line sketched nearly vertical is constrained to be vertical. The factor that determines how near to vertical a line has to be is the sketch angle tolerance. If a line falls within the determined angular tolerance, it will be constrained to be vertical; if it does not, no constraint is added. All of the sketching rules have similar tolerances, yet these tolerances may be changed at any time through AutoCAD Designer's system variable options. All of the sketching rules are further explained in Chapter 2. In this chapter, we will assume the default settings for all **system variables**.

To create the bookshelf, we want to start by creating a sketch for the **base feature**. A base feature is always the first three-dimensional feature created for a **part**. Every time a new part is created, a new base feature is also created. A base feature is the foundation for a final model design. All secondary features of the model are built around this foundation.

Helpful Hint: Keep your base feature as simple as possible to ease editing when the model becomes more complex.

Our simplest base feature is a rectangle defined by the length and height of the book-shelf. This shape can define the overall model fully while maintaining its simplicity. The rectangle is shown in Figure 1–2. Remember, this sketch is rough and does not need to be precise.

Figure 1-2

Helpful Hint: Draw your sketch at approximately its true size. This practice helps to prevent unexpected results when constraining a profile.

A sketch is always drawn on the **active sketch plane**. A **sketch plane** is fully defined by an infinite plane in space and an x- and y-axis orientation. Sketch planes help to simplify the modeling process by allowing most of a feature to be defined in two-dimensional space. Only the creation of a feature adds the third dimension. By default, the sketch plane for the base feature is the **world coordinate system** (WCS) XY plane. If a sketch plane other than the WCS XY plane is required for the base feature, simply use the **ADSKPLN** command to redefine the plane before drawing the base-feature sketch.

Once a sketch is created on a sketch plane, the next step is to inform AutoCAD Designer that this sketch is to become a profile. **Profiles** can be extruded, revolved, or swept along a path to become a **feature**. AutoCAD Designer's **ADPROFILE** command allows a sketch consisting of a set of lines and arcs to be interpreted with the sketching rules. After a sketch is interpreted, AutoCAD Designer informs you how many constraints were assumed and how many constraints/**dimensions** are still needed to fully constrain the profile. A **fully constrained profile** contains all the information that is needed to fully define that profile; it cannot be interpreted in any other way. For example, a rectangular profile cannot be fully constrained by just two **vertical constraints** and two **horizontal constraints**. Even adding a width dimension does not fully constrain a rectangle. A rectangular profile is not fully constrained until a length dimension is used in conjunction with a width dimension, two vertical constraints, and two horizontal constraints.

Profiles can also be constrained using **global parameters**. Global parameters are dimensional equations. These equations can be either stand alone parameters such as width = 36 or relational parameters such as height = width * 2. Global parameters are defined using the **ADPARAM** command and may be redefined at any time during the modeling process. A list of global parameters can be made universal for a series of drawings by exporting the list to a separate file and then importing the list into other drawings. To design the bookshelf the following global parameters were defined:

width = 30

thickness = 1.5

height = width * 2

depth = 12

shelf_depth = depth – thickness * 2

Any combination of constraints, dimensions, and global parameters can be used to fully constrain a profile. Figure 1–3 shows the fully constrained profile used for the bookshelf.

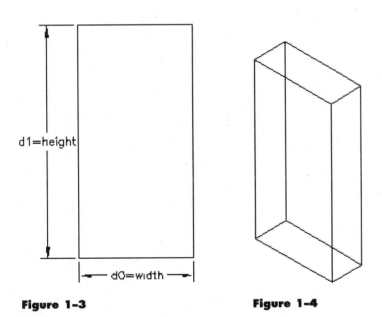

Figure 1-3   **Figure 1-4**

Helpful Hint: Although a profile does not need to be fully constrained to become a feature, we highly recommend that you take the extra time to fully constrain all profiles. A fully constrained profile requires less interpretation by AutoCAD Designer and maintains accurate updating with no guesswork.

A fully constrained profile can be extruded, revolved, or swept to become a feature. The first feature that is needed for our bookshelf is an **extrusion**. An extrusion projects a profile a specified distance along the z-axis as defined by the sketch plane. **Draft angles** can also be specified when creating an extrusion. A draft angle is defined as the angle of tapering, either positive or negative, applied to a feature. Although many models incorporate draft angles into their design, no draft angle is necessary for our bookshelf. We use the **ADEXTRUDE** command to turn our fully constrained profile into an extruded feature. An extrusion distance can be defined by either a numerical value or a global parameter. In this case, we defined the extrusion distance by the global parameter depth. When viewed from an isometric viewpoint, the extruded profile resembles Figure 1–4.

AutoCAD Designer always displays the model as if it were transparent. This display resembles that of a wireframe, although all AutoCAD Designer models are solid. Unfortunately, AutoCAD's HIDE command does not work on AutoCAD Designer models unless they are meshed. (The mesh procedure is discussed later in the book.) For now try to visualize the models with their transparent properties. To ease this learning process, throughout the book certain figures include a Hidden view representation in addition to the Transparent view representation.

The next modeling step is to begin to build upon the base feature. As subsequent features are made, they begin to shape the model into its final design. Each feature needs a newly defined and constrained profile on a specified sketch plane. The next feature hollows out the inside of our bookshelf to resemble a bookshelf without any shelves. The simplest option for defining our required sketch plane is to use the front surface of the model, as illustrated by the dashed lines in Figure 1–5. The x- and y-axis orientation is also shown in Figure 1–5.

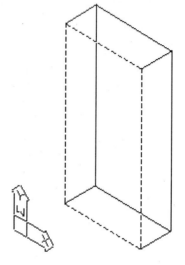

Figure 1–5

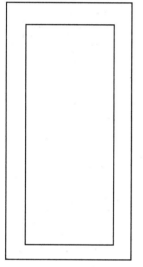

Figure 1–6

Now that the sketch plane is defined, a new profile needs to be sketched. For sketching purposes, a part may be viewed from any orthographic orientation or by views of Isometric and Sketch. A Sketch view views the part from an orientation that is perpendicular to the sketch plane no matter where that plane is defined. For the bookshelf the needed geometry is again rectangular in shape. After switching to a Sketch plane view, AutoCAD Designer uses ADPROFILE to interpret the rectangle drawn inside the base feature. (see Figure 1–6).

Because the next profile does not define a base feature, it needs two additional parameters, either constraints, dimensions, or global parameters, to fully constrain it. These two additional parameters need to define the new profile to the base feature in an X distance and a Y distance. The Z distance is automatically defined by the location of the sketch plane. To fully constrain our sketch, we will be using the global parameter thickness to maintain a constant wall between the outside and inside of the bookshelf. When it is fully constrained, the profile will resemble Figure 1–7.

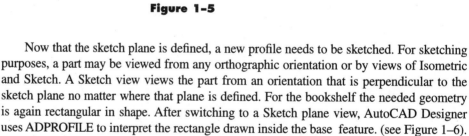

Helpful Hint: Before creating a feature, change to an Isometric orientation, which will allow you to select the feature-placement direction correctly.

After switching to an Isometric view, our fully constrained profile was extruded to a distance of depth – thickness inward toward the part. At this stage in the modeling process

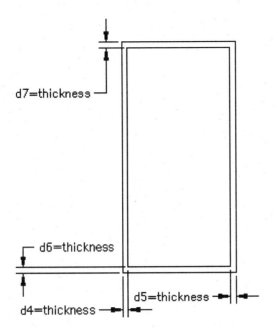

Figure 1-7

our bookshelf resembles the drawing in Figure 1–8. Remember that although you are seeing the part transparently, you are actually looking at a solid model.

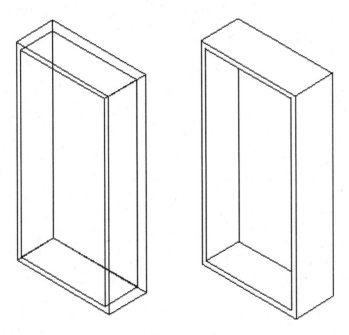

Figure 1-8

The next three features that need to be created for this part are the shelves. Each shelf is a separate feature and requires its own separately constrained profile. Of course, our active sketch plane must be defined first. Bookshelves are placed against the inside-back surface of a bookcase; therefore, this is the surface we wish to sketch on, and our profiles will be extruded toward the front of the bookcase to create the shelves. After defining the inside-back surface as the active sketch plane we switch the view orientation to Sketch view and draw three rough sketches to represent the approximate placement of the shelves. See Figure 1–9.

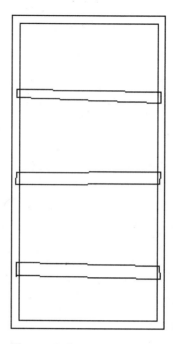

Figure 1-9

Helpful Hint: Although there can be only one active sketch at a time, more than one rough sketch may be drawn on an active sketch plane at any time. This practice is extremely useful when you have identical features such as the book shelves. Although AutoCAD Designer's features cannot be copied, a sketch can be copied to save time.

The ADPROFILE command is used to make one of the sketches the **active profile**. This profile is fully constrained with a combination of constraints, dimensions, and global parameters. Besides the horizontal and vertical constraints that are assumed, we add two **collinear constraints** to the sides of the shelf to make it the same width as the inside of

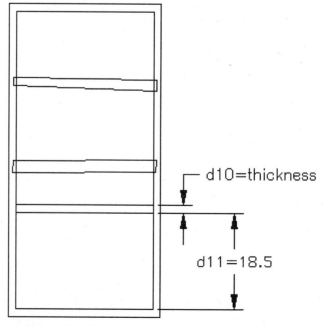

Figure 1-10

the bookcase. A collinear constraint relates two different lines by making them in line with each other. Next, the global parameter thickness is added to define the width of the shelf. Finally, we add a dimension to define the height of the shelf relative to the bottom of the bookcase. The fully dimensioned profile is shown in Figure 1–10 (see page 6). Take note that constraints are not represented in Figure 1–10. Constraints need to be displayed separately using the **ADSHOWCON** command if you wish to view them. Constraints are explained in detail in Chapter 2.

Since this profile is now fully constrained, it can be extruded to create the first shelf feature. Remember to switch to an Isometric view before creating a feature to see the feature-placement direction. For our bookcase we wish to extrude the shelf a distance equal to the global parameter shelf_depth. At this stage our part looks like the drawing in Figure 1–11.

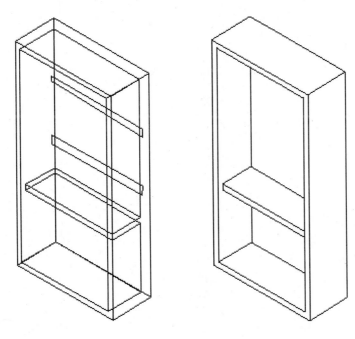

Figure 1-11

The other two shelves are created in the same manner. First, the sketch is made active by creating a profile. Next, the profile is fully constrained. Finally, the fully constrained profile is extruded to create a feature. After all three shelves have been created, the part resembles the drawing in Figure 1–12.

As mentioned before, parametric modeling is a two-way process. Now that our feature base model is created, we have the option of making changes. This option is especially useful when a model is still in the design stage and final dimensions are not yet known. Suppose we decided to redefine the width parameter of our bookcase at 45 inches instead of 30 inches; we decide to keep the height at 60 inches. The global parameter width needs to be recreated to width = 45. If we display a list of the global parameters at this time, it would show height = width * 2. If we do not change this equation, the corresponding height will be 90 inches, which is incorrect. Therefore, we also need to redefine the height parameter at height = 60. After these global parameters are redefined, the model needs to be updated. Figure 1–13 shows our updated bookcase, with the redefined global parameters.

Another handy feature of AutoCAD Designer is the automatic creation of drawing views. View types such as Orthographic, Sectional, Auxiliary, Detail, and Isometric are added to a drawing in **Paper space**. Paper space is also referred to as **Drawing mode**. Throughout this book we use these terms interchangeably. AutoCAD Designer can add dimensions to these drawing views automatically when the ADREUSEDIM system variable is set to 1. Once created, these dimensions can be moved, frozen/thawed, or deleted with ease.

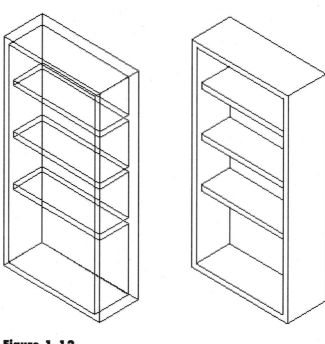

Figure 1-12

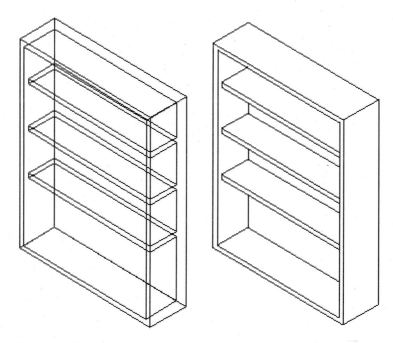

Figure 1-13

Helpful Hint: Changes made to the ADREUSEDIM variable affect only the drawing views created after the variable is changed. Previously created views are not affected.

You can also insert title blocks into Paper space to give your drawing a professional appearance. You have the option of using either AutoCAD's standard title blocks or creating custom title blocks. Drawing views of our bookshelf were created using AutoCAD

Designer's automatic dimensioning, and a standard AutoCAD title block was also insert-
ed into our drawing. The resulting drawing is shown in Figure 1–14.

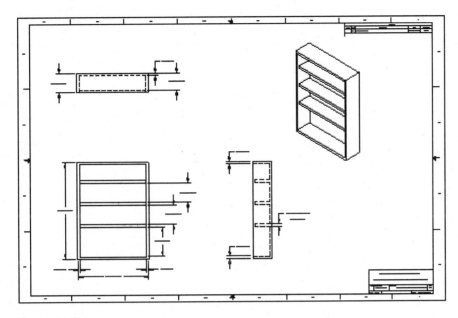

Figure 1-14

Finished models have many uses, most of which require transferring your model data
into various formats. Specific files can be made for applications such as CNC machining,
StereoLithography prototyping, and certain software packages such as AutoSurf® or
AutoVision™.

In some circumstances you may want to transfer your model to a three-dimensional
assembly drawing. Three-dimensional assembly drawings convey how different parts mate
and work together. It is unusual to have a part work independently, but note that the mating
part can be as simple as a washer to create an assembly. For our bookshelf assembly, we
added a rubber ball and a jump rope. Even though these might not be considered mating
parts, perhaps the bookshelf will go in a child's bedroom where these items might be placed

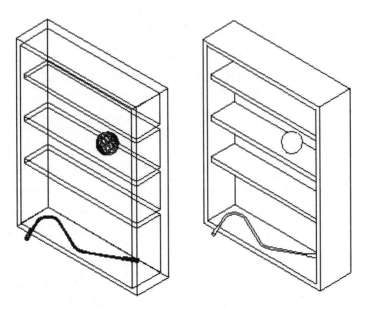

Figure 1-15

upon it; thus, the unit is an assembly. A two-dimensional drawing can even be made of the assembly in the same manner that one was created for a single model. Figures 1–15 and 1–16 show the three-dimensional and two-dimensional assembly data, respectively. Automatic dimensioning was turned off before the creation of the two-dimensional assembly.

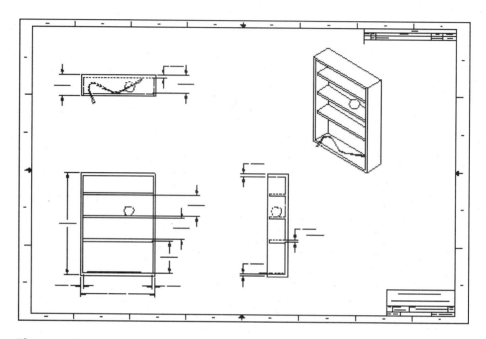

Figure 1–16

Our rubber ball was created using AutoCAD Designer's ADREVOLVE command. A revolve may be thought of as a profile rotated around a specific axis. Chapter 5 explains the **revolution** process. The jump rope was created with two different processes. A profile was swept along a path to create the rope feature, and then two separate extrusions were made to create the handle features. For a detailed explanation of the **sweep** process refer to Chapter 6.

As you will learn, AutoCAD Designer is a complete modeling package. With a little practice, intuition, and patience, you can create any design you can imagine. Have fun!

REVIEW QUESTIONS

1.1   Name six different types of features.

1.2   How many times per part does a base feature need to be created?

1.3   How do sketch planes help to simplify the modeling process?

1.4   Name the six parameters that are needed to fully constrain a rectangular profile for a base feature. What two additional parameters are needed if the rectangular profile is used for a secondary feature and not a base feature?

1.5   Name the three parameter methods that can be used together to obtain a fully constrained profile.

1.6   Why should you always fully constrain a profile?

1.7   What advantage is there to switching to an Isometric view before creating a feature?

1.8   How many active sketches can you have at one time?

1.9   List five different types of drawing views that can be created in Drawing mode by AutoCAD Designer.

1.10 What is the purpose of an assembly drawing?

chapter

2

SKETCHING

Before creating geometric features, you need to begin with a two-dimensional sketch. This sketch is meant to resemble a hand-drawn paper sketch. Lines need not be perfectly straight and endpoints of lines need not quite touch, yet someone looking at the piece of paper could interpret the sketch and form a clear mental picture of what it represents. AutoCAD Designer can make this same type of interpretation. The ADPROFILE command will interpret and clean up the rough sketch, allowing you then to add exact dimensions and additional constraints to solve the sketch fully. The sketching rules that AutoCAD Designer follows when interpreting your sketch follow in order, along with the default settings:

- Lines sketched nearly horizontal are made horizontal (within ±4 degrees from the horizontal).
- Lines sketched nearly vertical are made vertical (within ±4 degrees from the vertical).
- Lines, arcs, or circles sketched nearly tangent with one another are made tangent (within the current pickbox size).
- Arcs or circles whose centers are sketched nearly coincident with one another are made concentric (within the current pickbox size).
- Lines sketched nearly overlaying each other along the same line are made collinear (within the current pickbox size).
- Lines sketched nearly parallel with each other are made parallel (within the current pickbox size).
- Lines with attached endpoints sketched nearly perpendicular with each other are made perpendicular (within the current pickbox size).
- Objects with the endpoint near a point of another object are made attached to each other (within the current pickbox size).

After a sketch is interpreted by AutoCAD Designer, you can view all of the constraints applied to the sketch by using the ADSHOWCON command. Constraints can be deleted using **ADDELCON.** Additional constraints can be added using **ADADDCON.** You can change all of AutoCAD Designer's sketching system variables by using the **ADSET-TINGS** command, or you can turn off AutoCAD Designer's automatic interpretation of a rough sketch by using the ADSETTINGS command. All of these commands will be further explained in this chapter.

ADPROFILE

After the two-dimensional rough sketch is created, ADPROFILE is used to turn the selected geometry into an active sketch with the preceding rules applied to it. This active sketch, which is used as a cross-sectional profile, will later be extruded, revolved, or swept along a path to create a three-dimensional feature.

Command: **adprofile**

Select objects for sketch: *Select a two-dimensional sketch.*

Use the default settings and the ADPROFILE command to "clean up" the two-dimensional sketch. A nearly horizontal line is made horizontal or a line that is nearly tangent with a mating arc is made tangent. Use the cursor crosshairs for reference when sketching. These assumptions enable you to create your sketch quickly without spending a lot of time on detail or precision. The precision will come later after constraining and/or dimensioning the newly created profile. Figure 2-1 shows how the ADPROFILE command transforms a rough sketch into an active profile.

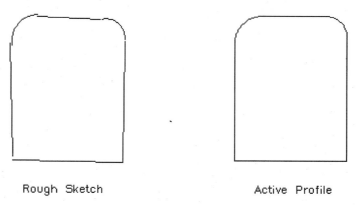

Rough Sketch   Active Profile

Figure 2-1

ADPROFILE TUTORIAL

The following tutorial explains how the ADPROFILE command interprets the rough sketch shown in Figure 2–1.

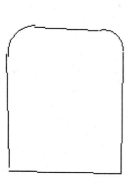

Figure 2-2

1. Start a new drawing in AutoCAD Designer and name it sketch1.

    Command: **new**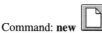

    Type **sketch1** in the New Drawing Name edit box.

    Choose **OK.**

2. Create your Scrap layer as described in Appendix A.

3. Set Scrap as your current layer.

4. Draw a rough sketch similar to that shown in Figure 2–2 using AutoCAD's line and arc commands.

5. Make the sketch into an active profile.

    Command: **adprofile**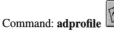

    Select objects for sketch.

    Select objects: *Select the entire rough sketch.*

    Select objects: ↵

    Solved under constrained sketch requiring 4 dimensions/constraints.

    If your last message showed that the number of dimensions/constraints needed was greater than four, AutoCAD Designer did not assume every constraint. This problem could result if some of your sketched lines were outside of the default system variable settings; for example, if your horizontal line was sketched at 5 degrees, AutoCAD Designer did not assume that it was horizontal. If you do require more dimensions/constraints than four, restart this tutorial at the beginning and use the cursor crosshairs as a reference when sketching. Continue to repeat this tutorial until you require only four dimensions/constraints after using the ADPROFILE command.

6. Save your work.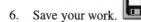

ADSHOWCON

After the active profile or path is created, ADSHOWCON can be used to display the existing constraints on the active sketch. Constraints are a method of defining your geometry. They can be used to specify horizontal or vertical lines, tangencies, collinearity, and other constraints. Figure 2–3 shows an example of an active sketch with all constraints displayed.

Helpful Hint: If you display the existing constraints before you add new dimensions and/or constraints, you will know AutoCAD Designer's current assumptions.

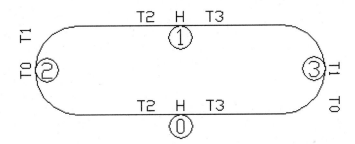

Figure 2-3

When showing what constraints exist on which entities, AutoCAD Designer uses symbols to identify the various constraints. A circled number near each **entity** identifies that entity. Opposite the entity number is a list of all constraints applied to that entity. For example, T3 means that this entity is tangent with entity number 3. Table 2–1 gives a complete listing of AutoCAD Designer constraints and their symbols.

Table 2-1

Constraint	Symbol
Horizontal	H
Vertical	V
Perpendicular	L
Parallel	P
Collinear	C
Concentric	N
Projected	J
Same as Radius	R
Tangent	T
Same as X	X
Same as Y	Y

A brief description of each constraint follows.

Horizontal   A line that is horizontal is parallel to the x-axis. A single line in your sketch needs to be picked to add a horizontal constraint.

Vertical   A line that is vertical is parallel to the y-axis. A single line in your sketch needs to be picked to add a vertical constraint.

Perpendicular   Two lines that are perpendicular lie 90 degrees apart from one another. Two different lines need to be selected to add a **perpendicular constraint,** and no more than one of them can be on your model.

Parallel   Two lines that are **parallel** have the same slope. Two different lines need to be selected to add a **parallel constraint,** and no more than one of them can be on your model.

Tangent   Two objects are tangent if at their intersection point they have the same slope. Tangency can occur between a pair of arcs or circles or between a line and an arc or circle, but never between a pair of lines. Two different objects need to be selected to add a **tangent constraint,** and one of these must be an arc or circle. Again, no more than one of the objects picked can be on your model.

Collinear   Two lines that are collinear are parallel and lie on the same infinite line. It is not required that they have the same endpoints. Two different lines need to be selected to add a collinear constraint, and no more than one of them can be on your model.

Concentric   Two circles or arcs that are concentric have the same center point. Two different arcs or circles need to be selected to add a **concentric constraint,** and no more than one of them can be on your model.

Projected   The **projected constraint** projects the endpoint of a line or the center point of an arc or circle onto another line. To use this constraint, first pick the line, arc, or circle that you want to project and then pick the line that you want to project the entity onto. (Note: The source object must be part of the active sketch, but the target object can be either on the active sketch or on the model).

Join   The **join constraint** closes the gap between the endpoints of two entities. Select the endpoint of one line or arc to join and another arc or line endpoint. No more than one of the endpoints can be on your model.

XValue   Two circles or arcs can have an **XValue constraint** if their center points have the same X coordinate. To apply this constraint, two different arcs or circles need to be selected with no more than one of them being on the model.

Yvalue   Two circles or arcs can have a **Yvalue constraint** if their center points have the same Y coordinate. To apply this constraint, two different arcs or circles need to be selected with no more than one of them being on the model.

Radius   Two arcs or circles that have the **radius constraint** added to them will have the same radius. Two different arcs or circles, one of which must already be dimensioned, need to be selected to add a radius constraint, and no more than one of the arcs or circles can be from the model.

Command: **adshowcon**

All/Select/Next/<eXit>: *Choose an option depending on which constraints you wish to see.*

All   Displays all existing constraints in the active sketch.

Select   Displays only the constraints of entities you select in the active sketch.

Next   When several constraints overlap each other, this option is helpful as it allows you to display constraints on specified entities one at a time.

> Select Constraint/eXit/<Next>: *Choose an option.*
>
> **Select Constraint**   Highlights an entity based on the constraint chosen.
>
> **Exit**   Returns to the previous constraint options.
>
> **Next**   Cycles to the next entity.

ADSHOWCON TUTORIAL

The following tutorial covers how to display AutoCAD Designer constraints.

1. Open your sketch1 drawing.

Command: **open**

Open sketch1.dwg by selecting the drive and directory of the file and then selecting the file.

Choose OK.

2. Show all the active constraints applied to your sketch.

    Command: **adshowcon**

    All/Select/Next/<eXit>: **a**

    Your screen should resemble Figure 2–4.

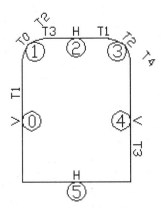

Figure 2–4

You will notice from Figure 2–4 that AutoCAD Designer assumed eight constraints. These constraints are, by entity:

Entity 0 is vertical and tangent to entity 1.

Entity 1 is tangent to entities 0 and 2.

Entity 2 is horizontal and tangent to entities 1 and 3.

Entity 3 is tangent to entities 2 and 4.

Entity 4 is vertical and tangent to entity 3.

Entity 5 is horizontal.

As you can see, some constraints are listed twice, such as the tangency assumed between entities 0 and 1 is listed as T1 on entity 0 and T0 on entity 1. This will be the case for all constraints with the exception of horizontal and vertical.

Your entities may be numbered differently depending on the order in which they were drawn. When this chapter refers to an entity number, compare the entity of Figure 2–4 with the same entity of your sketch. Do not assume your entities to be numbered in the same manner.

3. Let's practice other ways to show constraints. This time we'll use the select option.

    All/Select/Next/<eXit>: **s**

    Select items in active sketch.

    Select objects: *Select both arcs.*

    Select objects: ↵

    Now only the constraints applied to the two selected arcs are shown (see Figure 2–5).

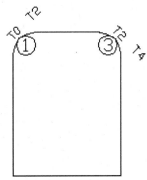

Figure 2–5

Helpful Hint: If you drew your sketch using the pline command, the select option will show the same results as the all option.

---

4. Now let's use the next option.

    All/Select/Next/<eXit>: **n**

    Select sketch items.

Select objects: *Select the entire profile.*

Select objects: ↵

This time constraints are displayed on only one entity at a time as shown in Figure 2–6. Use next to cycle to the next entity.

Select constraint/eXit/<Next>: **n**

Continue cycling through the entities until the left arc is displayed.

Helpful Hint: The number of entities in the cycle depends on the number of entities you selected at the Select objects prompt.

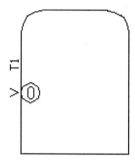

Figure 2-6

5. Now let's use the select constraint option.

    Select constraint/eXit/<Next>: **s**

    Select constraint: *Select the T0 constraint.*

    Your screen should now resemble Figure 2–7. Notice how the vertical line is highlighted along with the arc. This shows you which entity is being referred to in T0.

6. Exit the ADSHOWCON command.

    Select constraint/eXit/<Next>: **x**

    All/Select/Next/<eXit>: **x**

7. It is not necessary to save your work.

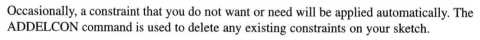

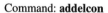

ADDELCON

Occasionally, a constraint that you do not want or need will be applied automatically. The ADDELCON command is used to delete any existing constraints on your sketch.

Command: **addelcon**

All/Select item to edit: *Choose an option.*

All   Deletes all constraints currently placed on entities in the active sketch.

Select Item to Edit   First displays the constraints on the selected entity and then deletes the symbol you choose from the entity.

ADDELCON TUTORIAL

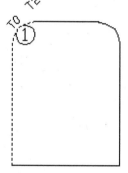

Figure 2-7

The following tutorial goes through the process of deleting constraints from an active sketch.

1. Open your sketch1 drawing.

    Command: **open**

    Open sketch1.dwg by selecting the drive and directory of the file and then selecting the file.

    Choose **OK.**

2. Delete both tangent constraints from entity 1, the left arc.

    Command: **addelcon**

    All/Select item to edit: **s**

    Select item to edit: *Select entity 1.*

    Select constraint to remove: *Select the T0 constraint.*

    Solved under constrained sketch requiring 5 dimensions/constraints.

    All/Select item to edit: **s**

Select item to edit: *Select entity 1.*

Select constraint to remove: *Select the T2 constraint.*

Solved under constrained sketch requiring 6 dimensions/constraints.

Note how the number of required dimensions/constraints rises every time a constraint is deleted.

3. Delete all remaining constraints from the sketch.

    All/Select item to edit: **a**

    Remove all constraints from active sketch Yes/<No>: **y**

    Solved under constrained sketch requiring 12 dimensions/constraints.

    All constraints removed from sketch.

4. Save your drawing as sketch2.

    Command: **saveas**

    Type in **sketch2** in the edit box.

    Choose **OK.**

ADADDCON

The ADADDCON command allows you to place relationships between your part geometry and the active sketch. Any of the constraints listed in Table 2–1 can be added.

Command: **adaddcon**

Hor/Ver/PErp/PAr/Tan/CL/CN/PRoj/Join/XValue/Yvalue/Radius/<eXit>: *Choose an option.*

Of the 11 constraints available, many have more than one usage. Five constraints, horizontal, vertical, parallel, perpendicular, and collinear, allow you to place relationships on lines. Parametric relationships with circles or arcs can be made with constraints such as radius, concentric, tangent, same X, and same Y. It is also possible to place constraints between your active sketch and model. This relationship can be achieved with any of the constraint options except horizontal and vertical.

Helpful Hint: Perpendicular constraints do not need to be added between vertical and horizontal lines. This constraint is automatic.

ADADDCON TUTORIAL

This tutorial shows how to add constraints to an active sketch.

1. Open your sketch2 drawing.

    Command: **open**

    Open sketch2.dwg by selecting the drive and directory of the file and then selecting the file.

    Choose **OK.**

2. Since we previously deleted all constraints from this sketch "by accident," now let's practice adding them back in. First add the horizontal constraints on entities 2 and 5; refer to Figure 2–4.

    Command: **adaddcon**

    Hor/Ver/PErp/PAr/Tan/CL/CN/PRoj/Join/XValue/Yvalue/Radius/<exit>: **h**

    Select line: *Select entity 2.*

    Solved under constrained sketch requiring 11 dimensions/constraints.

Hor/Ver/PErp/PAr/Tan/CL/CN/PRoj/Join/XValue/Yvalue/Radius/<eXit>: **h**

Select line: *Select entity 5.*

Solved under constrained sketch requiring 10 dimensions/constraints.

Note how the number of required dimensions/constraints decreases every time a constraint is added.

3. Next add the vertical constraints on entities 0 and 4.

Hor/Ver/PErp/PAr/Tan/CL/CN/PRoj/Join/XValue/Yvalue/Radius/<eXit>: **v**

Select line: *Select entity 0.*

Solved under constrained sketch requiring 9 dimensions/constraints.

Hor/Ver/PErp/PAr/Tan/CL/CN/PRoj/Join/XValue/Yvalue/Radius/<eXit>: **v**

Select line: *Select entity 4.*

Solved under constrained sketch requiring 8 dimensions/constraints.

4. The last step is adding tangencies between the arcs and their adjoining lines.

Hor/Ver/PErp/PAr/Tan/CL/CN/PRoj/Join/XValue/Yvalue/Radius/<eXit>: **t**

Select first item to make tangent: *Select entity 1, the left arc.*

Select second item to be tangent to first: *Select entity 0, the left vertical line.*

Solved under constrained sketch requiring 7 dimensions/constraints.

Hor/Ver/PErp/PAr/Tan/CL/CN/PRoj/Join/XValue/Yvalue/Radius/<eXit>: **t**

Select first item to make tangent: *Select entity 1 again.*

Select second item to be tangent to first: *Select entity 2, the upper horizontal line.*

Solved under constrained sketch requiring 6 dimensions/constraints.

Hor/Ver/PErp/PAr/Tan/CL/CN/PRoj/Join/XValue/Yvalue/Radius/<eXit>: **t**

Select first item to make tangent: *Select entity 3, the right arc.*

Select second item to be tangent to first: *Select entity 2, the upper horizontal line.*

Solved under constrained sketch requiring 5 dimensions/constraints.

Hor/Ver/PErp/PAr/Tan/CL/CN/PRoj/Join/XValue/Yvalue/Radius/<eXit>: **t**

Select first item to make tangent: *Select entity 3 again.*

Select second item to be tangent to first: *Select entity 4, the right vertical line.*

Solved under constrained sketch requiring 4 dimensions/constraints.

Hor/Ver/PErp/PAr/Tan/CL/CN/PRoj/Join/XValue/Yvalue/Radius/<eXit>: **x**

Helpful Hint: When applying constraints between two entities, the order in which the entities are selected is irrelevant.

---

5. It is not necessary to save your work.

ADSETTINGS

ADSETTINGS allows you to change the AutoCAD Designer system variables.

Command: **adsettings**

The Designer Settings dialogue box is shown in Figure 2–8. **Every AutoCAD Designer system variable can be set from this dialogue box!**

Sketch Settings   Controls all of the AutoCAD Designer sketch variables.

Rule Mode   When the Rule mode system variable is turned off, the only constraint that is applied by AutoCAD Designer is the joining of entity endpoints. The command line

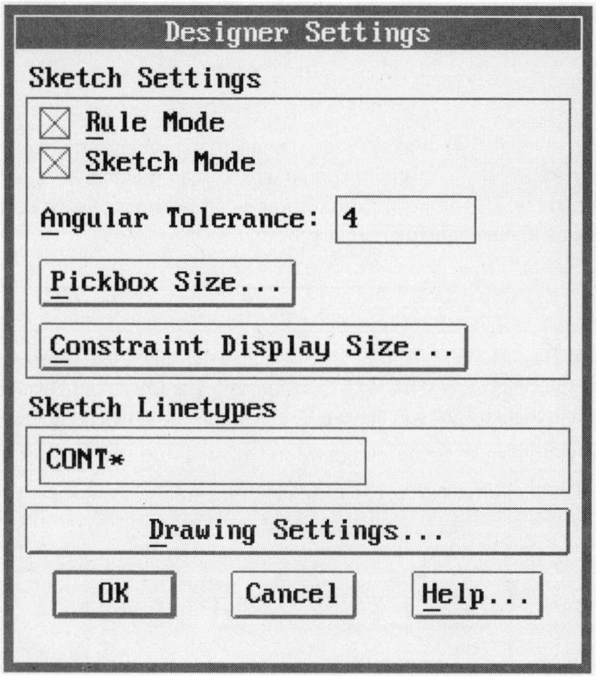

Figure 2-8

equivalent is ADRULEMODE, which accepts possible integer values of 1 or 0. The default value is 1, which means that constraints are automatically applied.

Sketch Mode   When the Sketch mode system variable is turned off, AutoCAD Designer does not apply any constraints to your sketch, allowing the sketch to be assumed precise as drawn. ADSKMODE is the command line equivalent. Possible integer values are again 1 or 0 with 1 being the default, meaning that AutoCAD Designer does apply all constraints.

Angular Tolerance   Controls the tolerance angle allowed for AutoCAD Designer to determine if a line should be constrained to be horizontal or vertical. Values between .001 and 10.0 are allowed. The command line equivalent is ADSKANGTOL with a default value of 4. This means that if in your sketch you drew a line at 3 degrees to the horizontal, AutoCAD Designer assumes this line to be horizontal; however, if you drew the same line at 5 degrees to the horizontal, AutoCAD Designer assumes that you meant it to be 5 degrees and will not apply a constraint to it.

Pickbox Size   Allows you to change the size of your pickbox from the dialogue box shown in Figure 2–9. Move the slide in the bar to determine the size.

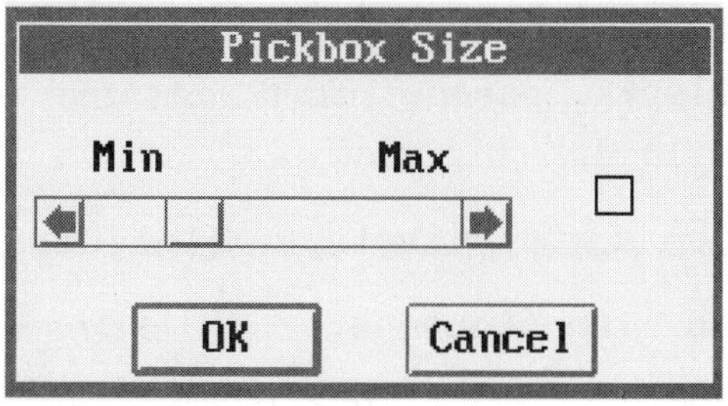

Figure 2-9

The size of your pickbox is a big factor in determining whether these constraints will be applied. For example, endpoints of lines and arcs will only be attached if their endpoints are both within the current pickbox size. If a geometry entity is smaller then your current pickbox size, AutoCAD Designer will ignore it.

Helpful Hint: Always take a second to check that the number of objects found is equal to the intended number of objects being selected. To avoid having AutoCAD Designer ignore small object entities, maintain a small pickbox size, and because your pickbox size is relative to the size of the screen and not your drawing, zoom in on your sketch geometry before selecting it. Zooming increases the relative size of your entities without changing the pickbox size.

Constraint Display Size   Allows you to change the height that constraints will be displayed when using the ADSHOWCON command. The Constraint Display Size dialogue box shown in Figure 2–10 will appear. Use the slide bar to determine the size of the display.

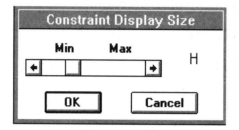

Figure 2-10

Helpful Hint: Try to maintain a small constraint size. If the constraint size is too large, the constraints will overlap and be unreadable.

Sketch Linetypes   Defines which linetype AutoCAD Designer will acknowledge as primary for a path or profile.

Drawing Settings   When the Drawing Settings button is picked the Drawing Variables dialogue box, shown in Figure 2–11, will appear. This is where you can set Drawing mode variables.

Drawing Variables
Projection type of unfolded views:
■ Third angle   □ First Angle
☒ Display parametric dimensions
☒ Hide drawing viewport borders
Section symbol linetype: PHANTOM2
Hidden line linetype: HIDDEN
OK   Cancel   Help...

Figure 2-11

ProjectionType of Unfolded Views   Selects which projection type you want to use on your drawing. Third-angle projection is the default value and the type of projection that is commonly used in the United States. First-angle projection is commonly used in the United Kingdom. The command line equivalent is ADPROJTYPE. Possible values are 1 and 0 with 1 being third-angle projection and the default value.

Display Parametric Dimensions   Allows you to choose whether AutoCAD Designer should display parametric dimensions as you create drawing views. The default value will display parametric dimensions. ADREUSEDIM is the command line equivalent. ADREUSEDIM accepts a value of 1 or 0 with 1 being the default value of displaying parametric dimensions. A change in this setting does not affect any existing views.

Hide Drawing Viewport Borders   Lets you determine whether AutoCAD Designer should display or hide the viewport borders as you create drawing views. The command line equivalent is ADBORDER with possible values of 1 or 0. A value of 1 is the default and hides the viewport borders.

Section Symbol Linetype   Allows you to set the linetype that will be used as section lines on the **parent view** of a cross-section. The phantom linetype is the default. ADSEC-LTYPE is the command line equivalent and accepts input of any valid AutoCAD linetype. A change in this setting does not affect any existing views.

Hidden Line Linetype   Sets the linetype that will be used to display hidden lines in a drawing view. The hidden linetype is the default value. The command line equivalent is ADHIDLTYPE, and it accepts input of any valid AutoCAD linetype. A change in this setting does not affect any existing views.

ADSETTINGS TUTORIAL

The following tutorial explains how various system variables affect the way AutoCAD Designer interprets a sketch.

1. Start a new drawing in AutoCAD Designer and name it sketch3.

    Command: **new**

    Type **sketch3** in the New Drawing Name edit box.

    Choose **OK.**

2. Create your Scrap layer as described in Appendix A.

3. Set Scrap as your current layer.

4. Use AutoCAD's line and arc commands to draw a rough sketch similar to that shown in Figure 2–12.

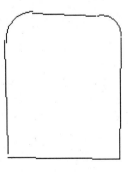

Figure 2-12

5. Let's mark this point so we can return to it later.

    Command: **undo**

    Auto/Back/Control/End/Group/Mark/<number>: **m**

6. Turn off ADRULEMODE to see the effect when ADPROFILE is used.

    Command: **adrulemode**

    New value for ADRULEMODE (1=assume on, 0=off) <1>: **0**

7. Turn the sketch into the active profile.

    Command: **adprofile**

    Select objects for sketch.

    Select objects: *Select the entire rough sketch.*

    Select objects: ↵

    Solved under constrained sketch requiring 12 dimensions/constraints.

    Your sketch should now resemble Figure 2–13.

Figure 2-13

Notice how only the endpoints of the entities were connected and no other constraints were assumed. In order for AutoCAD Designer to assume no constraints at all you need a combination of ADRULEMODE = 0 and ADSKMODE = 0. However, whenever ADSKMODE is set to 0, you need a continuous sketch with all endpoints connected; otherwise, AutoCAD Designer responds with "Unable to Construct Continuous Profile."

Helpful Hint: The best result is obtained if ADRULEMODE and ADSKMODE are set to 1, which allows AutoCAD Designer to assume all constraints. Do not waste time drawing your sketches precisely. Allow AutoCAD Designer to interpret them for you.

---

8. Let's return to the previous mark and re-mark that point.

    Command: **undo**

    Auto/Back/Control/End/Group/Mark/<number>: **b**

    Mark Encountered.

    Command: **undo**

    Auto/Back/Control/End/Group/Mark/<number>: **m**

9. Now, let's change the sketch angle tolerance.

    Command: **adskangtol**

    New value for ADSKANGTOL (.001 to 10.0 degrees) <4>: **0.5**

10. Again make a profile of your sketch.

Command: **adprofile**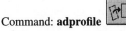

Select objects for sketch.

Select objects: *Select the entire rough sketch.*

Select objects: ↵

Solved under constrained sketch requiring 12 dimensions/constraints.

Were any constraints applied to your profile? Why or why not?

11. Let's return to the previous mark and re-mark that point.

Command: **undo**

Auto/Back/Control/End/Group/Mark/<number>: **b**

Mark Encountered.

Command: **undo**

Auto/Back/Control/End/Group/Mark/<number>: **m**

12. Now, let's make our pickbox extremely small. Remember, certain constraints will be applied only if they are within the pickbox size.

Command: **pickbox**

New value for PICKBOX <3>: **1**

13. Again make a profile of your sketch.

Command: **adprofile**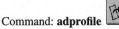

Select objects for sketch.

Select objects: *Select the entire rough sketch.*

Select objects: ↵

Unable to Construct Continuous Profile.

Have you figured out that AutoCAD Designer was unable to construct this profile because we decreased the size of our pickbox so it was virtually nonexistent? AutoCAD Designer would not apply endpoint constraints to join entities because the gap between them was larger than the pickbox size.

14. Save your work.

REVIEW QUESTIONS

2.1   Explain how to show all the constraints in an active sketch.

2.2   When applying constraints to a sketch, does AutoCAD Designer apply tangencies or parallelisms first?

2.3   What factor is involved when determining if a perpendicular constraint is to be applied?

2.4   What does it mean when an entity has an L2 constraint attached to it? How about X3?

2.5   How does deleting a constraint affect the number of dimensions/constraints that are required to fully constrain the sketch?

2.6   Is the order of the constraints relevant when applying constraints between two entities?

2.7   What effect does setting ADRULEMODE to 0 have on the ADPROFILE command?

2.8   Why is the pickbox size important?

CHAPTER EXERCISES

2.1   Roughly draw the shape shown in Figure Exer2–1. Make this into the active sketch using values of 1 for the ADRULEMODE and ADSKMODE system variables. List any constraints you think should be automatically assumed by AutoCAD Designer. Show all your constraints on your profile to verify your list. Save your work as Exer2-1.

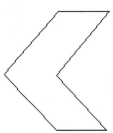

Figure Exer2-1

2.2   Open Exer2-1 and delete the parallel constraints applied to entities 1 and 2 as shown in Figure Exer2–2. Now add parallel constraints between entities 2 and 5 and between entities 1 and 4. How did this affect your profile geometry? Save your work as Exer2-2.

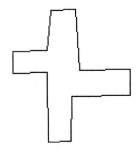

Figure Exer2-3

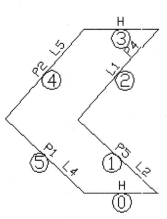

Figure Exer2-2

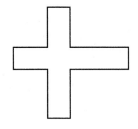

Figure Exer2-4

2.3   Draw the shape shown in Figure Exer2–3. Change the setting of the ADSKMODE system variable to 0 and create an active profile. Were any constraints applied? Why or why not?

Add all needed constraints to make the profile shown in Figure Exer2–3 resemble Figure Exer2–4. How many parameters are still needed to fully constrain the profile of Figure 2–4? (Hint: You should require six. Do you?)

2.4   Draw a hexagon inscribed inside a circle of hidden linetype as shown in Figure Exer2–5. Make a profile of these objects. Be sure to include the circle when selecting your sketch objects. Use an ADSKMODE setting of 1. Show all your constraints to see what happened. You should notice that six projection constraints have been added. The endpoints of the hexagon have been projected onto the circumference of the circle. The circle is considered construction geometry and reduces the total number of constraints/dimensions needed to fully constrain the sketch. With this construction circle the sketch needs three additional parameters. Without this construction circle, the sketch would need six additional parameters to be fully constrained. Save your work as Exer2-4.

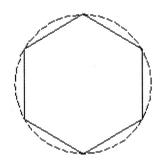

Figure Exer2-5

chapter

3

DIMENSIONS

This chapter contains several commands that are used to fully constrain a two-dimensional sketch, which will eventually become a solid feature. When a sketch is first created, it can be fairly rough and have an undefined geometry. After converting the sketch to a profile, AutoCAD Designer assumes certain parameters and leaves the rest undefined. A **fully constrained sketch** uses a combination of constraints, dimensions, and global parameters to define it; it requires no interpretation. In Chapter 2 you learned how to incorporate constraints into your sketch. This chapter shows you how to include dimensions and global parameters into your sketch to fully constrain it.

ADPARDIM

After you create an active sketch, your next goal is to fully constrain the sketch with dimensions and constraints before finally creating a feature for your model. Referring back to Chapter 2, the ADPROFILE command cleaned up your initial rough sketch. Now, the **ADPARDIM** command takes the active sketch one step further and allows you to change the sketch to match the exact dimensions you specify.

Unlike typical AutoCAD dimensioning, which is simply a visual representation of a standard parts drawing done on paper, the interactive ADPARDIM command creates dimension constraints that actually control the active sketch parametrically. When you place a parametric dimension, the active sketch changes to match that specified dimension. See Figure 3–1.

Original Active Sketch   Radial Dimension Added

Figure 3-1

Command: **adpardim**

Select first item: *Select an entity that you want to dimension.*

Select second item or place dimension: *Select a second entity if your dimension requires two or pick a location to place the dimension value.*

If you have a straight line dimension, the following prompt appears:

Undo/Hor/Ver/Align/Par/Dimension value <current>: *Choose an option or type in the dimension value.*

Undo   Performs a standard AutoCAD undo operation on the ADPARDIM command.

Hor   Makes the new dimension a horizontal dimension.

Ver   Makes the new dimension a vertical dimension.

Align   Aligns the dimension with your chosen points.

Par   Makes the new dimension a parallel dimension if parallel lines are selected.

Dimension Value   Accepts the specified value you entered.

If you have a circle or an arc dimension, the following prompt appears:

Undo/Dimension value <current>: *Enter an option.*

Undo   Performs a standard AutoCAD undo operation on the ADPARDIM command.

Dimension Value   Accepts the specified value you entered.

Helpful Hint: When selecting entities for dimensioning, AutoCAD Designer automatically selects the endpoints of lines and the centers of arcs/circles. There are no exceptions to this rule, not even with the use of AutoCAD snap commands.

The ADPARDIM command is capable of creating various types of dimensions. To create certain types of dimensions, you must follow AutoCAD Designer's rules and techniques:

Straight Line Dimensioning   For creating a linear dimension, there are several options. The recommended technique for aligned, parallel, horizontal, or vertical dimensions allows for fillets or chamfers to be added. This method is to pick two endpoints as shown in Figures 3–2 and 3–3 and may be required even if your dimension is not relating to a single straight line entity.

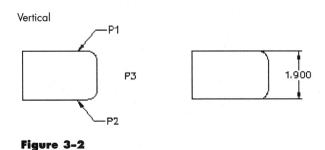

Figure 3-2

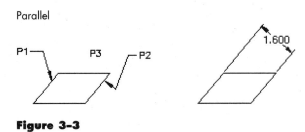

Figure 3-3

One other point to remember when adding dimensions is that edges of **work planes** made perpendicular to the active sketch can also be used for constraining your sketch as long as their display is on. A work plane is a reference plane defined by the user. Work planes are discussed further in Chapter 4.

A second and quicker method that applies to all of the linear dimensions (except parallel) is to pick the center of the line you wish to dimension as shown by P1 in Figures 3–4 and 3–5. This option is not valid if you are dimensioning between two entities.

Angular Dimensioning   Angular dimensions are slightly different than the standard straight line dimensions. One difference is that you must pick two nonparallel lines; the center point of a circle or an arc cannot be used. A second difference is that you must pick on the lines

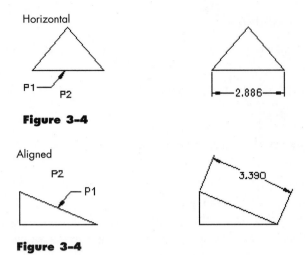

Figure 3-4

Figure 3-4

somewhere near the midpoints so that AutoCAD Designer recognizes that you are looking for an angular dimension, not a straight line dimension. See Figure 3–6.

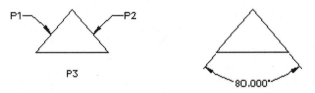

Figure 3-6

Circular Dimensioning   When dimensioning a circle or arc, AutoCAD Designer automatically assumes the center point for the pick point, no matter where you pick on the entity. If you select an arc, the dimension will be radial. For a circle, the dimension will be diametric. It is also possible to dimension between the center point of a circle or arc and another entity.

One other dimensioning technique to remember is that you can set dimensions equal to each other or you can relate one dimension to another with an equation, using either the Parameters or Equations display mode, which is explained later in this chapter.

The mathematical operators shown in Table 3–1 can also be used in equations.

Table 3-1

Operator	Description	Operator	Description
+	Addition	%	Modulus (remainder)
-	Subtraction	floor	Rounds down to the nearest integer
*	Multiplication	ceil	Rounds up to the nearest integer
/	Division	sin	Sine
( )	Parenthesis	cos	Cosine
^	Exponent of	tan	Tangent
sqrt	Square root of	asin	Arcsin ($\sin^{-1}$)
pi	pi	acos	Arccos ($\cos^{-1}$)
log	Logarithm of	atan	Arctan ($\tan^{-1}$)
ln	Natural logarithm of	sinh	Hyperbolic sine
e	Base number for natural logarithm	cosh	Hyperbolic cosine
exp(x)	e^x	tanh	Hyperbolic tangent

ADPARDIM TUTORIAL

The following tutorial covers the use of the ADPARDIM command to fully constrain the profile from Chapter 2.

1. Open the sketch1 drawing you created in Chapter 2.

    Command: **open**

    Open sketch1.dwg by selecting the drive and directory of the file and then selecting the file. Choose **OK.**

2. Create your Dimension and Model layers as described in Appendix A.

3. Set Dimension as your current layer.

4. Recall from Chapter 2 that this profile still requires four dimensions/constraints before it is fully constrained. Let's begin by dimensioning the overall length and height of the profile.

    Command: **adpardim**

    Select first item: *Pick P1 of Figure 3–7.*

    Select second item or place dimension: *Pick P2.*

    Undo/Hor/Ver/Align/Par/Dimension value <current>: **5.**↵

    Solved under constrained sketch requiring 3 dimensions/constraints.

    Select first item: *Pick P1 again.*

    Select second item or place dimension: *Pick P3.*

    Specify dimension placement: *Pick P4.*

    Undo/Hor/Ver/Align/Par/Dimension value <current>: **6.5.**↵

    Solved under constrained sketch requiring 2 dimensions/constraints.

    Select first item: ↵

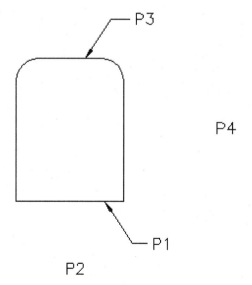

Figure 3-7

Notice how when we dimensioned the overall horizontal dimension, we needed only to select the line and then place the dimension. However, with the overall vertical dimension, we need to select two different entities because the fillet is part of the overall height. If we select only the vertical line and then place the dimension, we do not get an overall dimension.

5. We still require two dimensions/constraints to obtain a fully constrained profile. Let's dimension a fillet.

Command: **adpardim**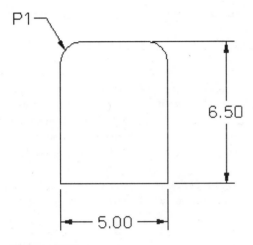

Select first item: *Select P1 of Figure 3–8.*

Select second item or place dimension: *Pick P2.*

Undo/Dimension value <current>: **1**↵

Solved fully constrained sketch.

Select first item: ↵

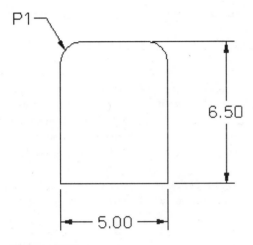

P1

6.50

5.00

Figure 3–8

Did you notice that by dimensioning just one fillet you added two constraints/dimensions? AutoCAD Designer assumed that you wanted the other fillet to be the same radius and hence added a radius constraint to it. A radius constraint is the only constraint option that is assumed after, not before, a dimension is added. If in fact you do not intend for these fillets to have the same radius, you can use the ADDELCON command described in Chapter 2 to eliminate the constraint. In that case you must dimension the second fillet in an additional step.

6. Save your work as Dim1.

Command: **saveas**

Type **dim1** in the edit box.

Choose **OK.**

ADFIXPT

The **ADFIXPT** command makes one point of the active sketch fixed on its position in the XYZ coordinate system relative to the remaining sketch entities. If the sketch is for a base feature, the fixed point becomes a three-dimensional holding point for the model in the WCS.

When creating a profile with the ADPROFILE command, a fixed point is automatically chosen depending on how your geometry was created. The ADFIXPT command simply gives you the option of specifying a new point for the active sketch. Figure 3–9 shows an example of the fixed point.

Command: **adfixpt**

Specify new fixed point for active sketch: *Select the point you want to be fixed.*

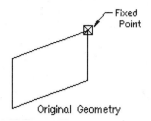
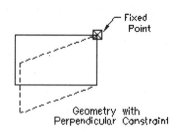

Figure 3-9

Helpful Hint: You do not need to use object snaps because AutoCAD Designer automatically picks endpoints of lines or center points of arcs and circles.

Depending on where your fixed point of the active sketch is positioned, you may find that some fixed-point locations make it easier for you to constrain the sketch than others. You may need to think about where this fixed-point location should be. When combining a fixed-point location with an inefficient dimension and constraint scheme, lines or other entities may end up crossing over each other, making it impossible to constrain your sketch properly.

As you can see in Figure 3–9, changes made to the sketch with new dimensions or constraints move the geometry to match the changes while keeping the fixed point in its original location.

ADFIXPT TUTORIAL

The following tutorial explains how the fixed point affects the sketch geometry.

1. Start a new drawing in AutoCAD Designer and name it dim2.

    Command: **new**

    Type **dim2** in the New Drawing Name edit box.

    Choose **OK.**

2. Create your Scrap layer as described in Appendix A.

3. Set Scrap as your current layer.

4. Create a parallelogram as shown in Figure 3–10 from the following information.

    Command: **line**

    From point: **5,5**

    To point: **@5<–30**

    To point: **@3<90**

    To point: **@5<150**

    To point: **c**

    For those who need a review, the preceding command sequence started a line from the X,Y coordinate of 5,5, drew a line with a length of 5 at an angle of –30 degrees, created a line from the previous endpoint with a length of 3 at an angle of 90 degrees, and then created a line with a length of 5 at an angle of 150 degrees. The line was closed to the original point.

5. Now copy the parallelogram so you have two parallelograms on the screen, as shown in Figure 3–11.

    Command: **copy**

    Select objects: *Select the four lines of the parallelogram.*

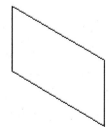

Figure 3-10

Select objects: ↵

<Base point or displacement>/Multiple: **0,0**

Second point of displacement: @**6,0**

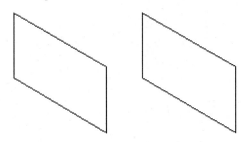

Figure 3-11

Two parallelograms will enable us to show the difference a fixed point location can make.

6. Make the first parallelogram into an active sketch.

Command: **adprofile**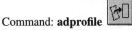

Select objects for sketch.

Select objects: *Select the first parallelogram.*

Select objects: ↵

Solved under constrained sketch requiring 3 dimensions/constraints.

7. Change the fixed point to be the upper-left corner.

Command: **adfixpt**

Specify new fixed point for active sketch: *Select the upper-left corner of the parallelogram.*

Solved under constrained sketch requiring 3 dimensions/constraints.

8. Now add a perpendicular constraint to any two adjacent sides.

Command: **adaddcon**

Hor/Ver/PErp/PAr/Tan/CL/CN/PRoj/Join/XValue/Yvalue/Radius/<eXit>: **pe**

Select first line: *Select any line of the active parallelogram.*

Select second line: *Select any adjacent line from the first line selected.*

Solved under constrained sketch requiring 2 dimensions/constraints.

Hor/Ver/PErp/PAr/Tan/CL/CN/PRoj/Join/XValue/Yvalue/Radius/<eXit>: ↵

Did you notice how your parallelogram was updated to reflect the perpendicular constraint placed upon it, while the fixed point remained stationary?

9. Do the same thing on the second parallelogram, but this time use the lower-right corner as the fixed point. Start with creating a profile.

Command: **adprofile**

Select objects for sketch.

Select objects: *Select the second parallelogram.*

Select objects: ↵

Solved under constrained sketch requiring 3 dimensions/constraints.

10. Change the fixed point to be the lower-right corner.

Command: **adfixpt**

Specify new fixed point for active sketch: *Select the lower-right corner of the parallelogram.*

Solved under constrained sketch requiring 3 dimensions/constraints.

11. Now add a perpendicular constraint to any two adjacent sides.

    Command: **adaddcon**

    Hor/Ver/PErp/PAr/Tan/CL/CN/PRoj/Join/XValue/Yvalue/Radius/<eXit>: **pe**

    Select first line: *Select any line of the active parallelogram.*

    Select second line: *Select any adjacent line from the first line selected.*

    Solved under constrained sketch requiring 2 dimensions/constraints.

    Hor/Ver/PErp/PAr/Tan/CL/CN/PRoj/Join/XValue/Yvalue/Radius/<eXit>: ⏎

    How did this parallelogram get shifted? Are the results the same? If everything went as planned, your screen should resemble Figure 3–12.

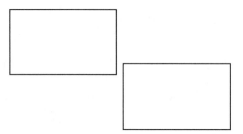

Figure 3-12

12. Save your work.

ADPARAM

The ADPARAM command lets you create, delete, list, export, and import global parameters used for dimensioning. With these global parameters you can define important or commonly used dimensions or you can even define equations with a mix of variables.

Command: **adparam**

Create/Delete/List/Import/Export/<eXit>: *Choose an option.*

Create   Enables you to make global parameters by assigning specific numbers or equations to them. Some examples of possible global parameters that you may want to create are shown in the following list.

Thickness = 0.25

Length = 10

Height = 5

Draft = 2

Support = height * cos(30)

Delete   Removes specified global parameters from the current drawing.

List   Displays the global parameters defined in the current drawing.

Import   Takes global parameters defined and exported from other drawings and brings them into the active drawing.

Export   Writes global parameters created in the current drawing to a .prm file so that they can be used in other drawing files.

When you add or change dimensions in the active sketch, you can enter global parameters at the Dimension value prompt of either the ADPARDIM or ADMODDIM commands. Simply type an equal sign followed by the parameter name.

You can change global parameters at any time by re-creating the parameter using the ADPARAM command and the create option.

> **Helpful Hint:** Dimension parameters, such as d1, d2, etc., and mathematical operators, as listed in Table 3–1, cannot be used as global parameter names.

ADPARAM TUTORIAL

The following tutorial repeats the ADPARDIM tutorial, but this time use global parameters to fully dimension the profile.

1. Open the sketch1 drawing you created in Chapter 2 and save it as dim3.

   Command: **open**

   Open sketch1.dwg by selecting the drive and directory of the file and then selecting the file.

   Choose **OK.**

   Command: **saveas**

   Type **dim3** in the edit box.

   Choose **OK.**

2. Create your Dimension and Model layers as described in Appendix A.

3. Set Dimension as your current layer.

4. Create the following global parameters:

   Width = 5.00

   Height = 6.50

   Radius = 1.00

   Command: **adparam**

   Create/Delete/List/Import/Export/<eXit>: **c**

   Enter equation: **width=5.00**

   Parameter "width" created: current value == 5.

   Enter equation: **length=6.50**

   Parameter "length" created: current value == 6.5.

   Enter equation: **radius=1.00**

   Parameter "radius" created: current value == 1.

   Enter equation: ↵

   Create/Delete/List/Import/Export/<eXit>: ↵

5. Recall from Chapter 2 that this profile still requires four dimensions/constraints before it is fully constrained. Now begin by dimensioning the overall length and height of the profile.

   Command: **adpardim**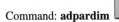

   Select first item: *Pick P1 of Figure 3–13.*

   Select second item or place dimension: *Pick P2.*

   Undo/Hor/Ver/Align/Par/Dimension value <current>: **width** ↵

   Solved under constrained sketch requiring 3 dimensions/constraints.

   Select first item: *Pick P1 again.*

   Select second item or place dimension: *Pick P3.*

   Specify dimension placement: *Pick P4.*

   Undo/Hor/Ver/Align/Par/Dimension value <current>: **height** ↵

   Solved under constrained sketch requiring 2 dimensions/constraints.

   Select first item: ↵

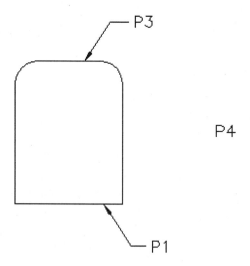

Figure 3-13

Did you notice that even though you entered global parameters, AutoCAD Designer continues to display the dimensions as numbers? We discuss dimension display options in the following section.

6. You still require two dimensions/constraints to obtain a fully constrained profile, so dimension the radii. Remember, by dimensioning one radius, AutoCAD Designer assumes the other.

Command: **adpardim**

Select first item: *Select P1 of Figure 3–14.*

Select second item or place dimension: *Pick P2.*

Undo/Dimension value <current>: **radius** ↵

Solved fully constrained sketch.

Select first item: ↵

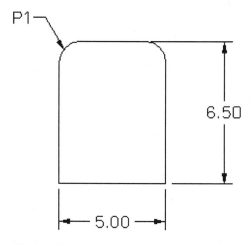

Figure 3-14

7. Do you have a fully constrained sketch? You should. Be sure to save your work.

ADDIMDSP

The **ADDIMDSP** command allows you to change the dimension display made to Numeric, Parameters, or Equations (see Figure 3–15). The last two display modes are useful when you want to base one dimension off of another. For instance, you may want the length of one line to equal that of another line, or you may want a radius to be two times that of another radius.

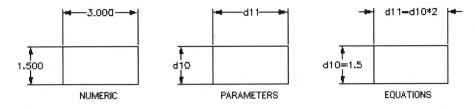

Figure 3-15

Command: **addimdsp**

Parameters/Equations/<Numeric>: *Enter a display mode.*

Parameters   Displays the dimension parameter symbol or name.

Equations   Displays the dimension parameter and the value or equation it is equal to.

Numeric   Displays only the numeric value for the dimension.

ADDIMDSP TUTORIAL

This tutorial walks you through AutoCAD Designer's various display methods.

1.   Open the dim3 drawing that you created earlier.

Command: **open**

Open dim3.dwg by selecting the drive and directory of the file and then selecting the file.

Choose **OK.**

2.   By default the dimension display is set to Numeric. Let's change it to Parameters.

Command: **addimdsp**

Parameters/Equations/<Numeric>: **parameters**

Your screen should now resemble Figure 3–16.

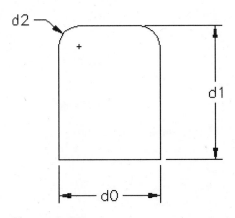

Figure 3-16

3.   View the Equations mode.

Command: **addimdsp**

Parameters/Equations/<Numeric>: **equations**

Your screen should now resemble Figure 3–17.

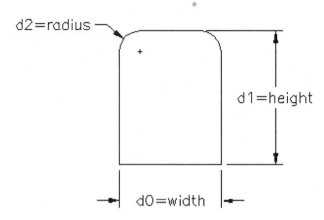

Figure 3-17

4.   Save your work.

ADMODDIM

The **ADMODDIM** command lets you change parametric dimension values on the active sketch or on the drawing views. ADMODDIM does not work on feature dimensions.

Command: **admoddim**

Select dimension to change: *Select the dimension you want to modify.*

New value for dimension <current>: *Type in the new dimension value or equation.*

ADMODDIM TUTORIAL

By the end of this tutorial, you will know how to edit dimensions on a sketch.

1.   Open your dim1 drawing and save it as dim4.

Command: **open**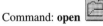

Open dim1.dwg by selecting the drive and directory of the file and then selecting the file.

Choose **OK.**

Command: **saveas**

Type **dim4** in the edit box.

Choose **OK.**

2.   Use the ADMODDIM command to change the overall width from 5.00 to 7.00.

Command: **admoddim**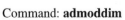

Select dimension to change: *Select the 5.00 dimension.*

New value for dimension <5.00>: **7.00**

Solved fully constrained sketch.

Select dimension to change: ↵

Your sketch should have been updated automatically and should now resemble Figure 3–18.

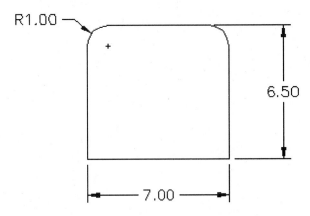

Figure 3-18

3. Save your work.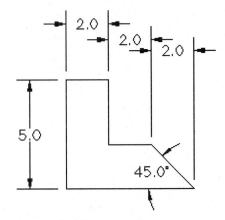

REVIEW QUESTIONS

3.1 When you use the ADPARDIM command, can you dimension from the quadrant of a circle? Why or why not?

3.2 How many lines have to be selected to add a parallel dimension?

3.3 Explain the difference between an aligned dimension and a parallel dimension.

3.4 How do you change the value of a global parameter?

3.5 How does the fixed point affect the active sketch when dimensioning?

3.6 Explain the three dimension display options and the differences between them.

3.7 What does the ADMODDIM command allow you to do?

CHAPTER EXERCISES

3.1 Draw the sketch shown in Figure Exer3–1 and use the dimensions provided to fully constrain it. Save your work as Exer3-1.

Figure Exer3-1

3.2   After creating the global parameters width = 4 and height = 5, draw and fully con-
        strain the object in Figure Exer3–2; use a combination of dimensions and global
        parameters. Save your work as Exer3-2 with the dimension display set to equa-
        tions. (Note: Assume tangencies.)

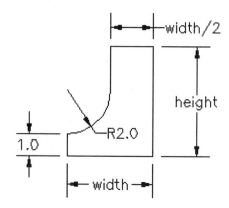

Figure Exer3-2

3.3   Open Exer3-1. Change your dimension display to Parameters. Now modify dimen-
        sions 2 and 3 in Figure Exer3–3 to be equal to dimension 1. For example, if dimen-
        sion 1 is d1, set dimension 2 equal to d1. Did this change affect your geometry?
        Why? Now change dimension 1 to 2.5. How many dimensions were affected by
        this change? Save your work as Exer3-3.

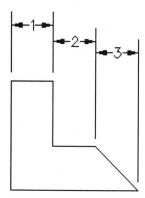

Figure Exer3-3

4

Extrusions and Planes

Geometric features constitute the heart of AutoCAD Designer. These are the features that can turn your two-dimensional profiles into three-dimensional solid models. These features can change your square into a block, your circle into the link of a chain, and your defined point into a drilled hole. This chapter covers only the extrude feature and some of the tools that perform a variety of extrusions. Learning all of the geometric features will allow you to design and create an unlimited number of complex, solid objects. Remember, you must be in Part mode to use the AutoCAD Designer feature commands.

ADEXTRUDE

The ADEXTRUDE feature performs two basic functions. The first of these is building a solid part that starts with a two-dimensional active profile, which you learned to create in Chapter 2. By pulling the sketch from the original flat plane into a third axis, you get a three-dimensional figure, as shown in Figure 4–1.

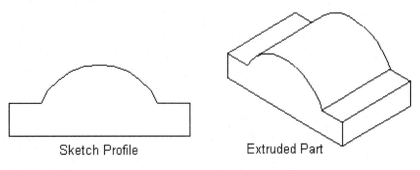

Sketch Profile   Extruded Part

Figure 4-1

In addition to being able to extrude a solid part by adding material, the ADEXTRUDE command can also cut away material from an existing solid object, as shown in Figure 4–2.

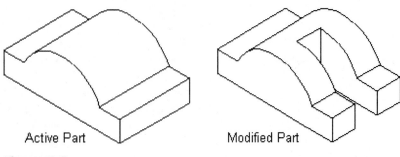

Active Part   Modified Part

Figure 4-2

Command: **adextrude**

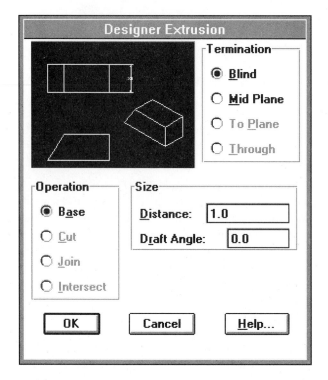

Figure 4–3

Operation   When the ADEXTRUDE command is used, the Designer Extrusion dialogue box appears, as shown in Figure 4–3. As you can see, you have several options to consider when making your extrusion. The first option determines the Operation.

    Base   The base is the foundation of your solid object. To create a new part, you must add material to create the base, or first feature, of the part.

    Cut   Cutting is the simplest way to remove material from the **active part**. This option cuts away notches, grooves, or channels.

    Join   The join option allows you to add material to an existing part. You can expand the active part as much as needed.

    Intersect   The intersect option removes any material from the active part that lies outside boundaries of where the new sketch is extruded. For example, if the active part is a cylinder and a larger box is extruded over the cylinder with the intersect option set, the active part does not change, as shown in Figure 4–4. However, if the sides of the box are slightly smaller than the existing cylinder, the round edges of the cylinder are trimmed to fit the box, as shown in Figure 4–5.

Termination   These four options provide different methods for determining the depth of your extruded sketch.

    Blind   The blind method of termination allows you to set a numeric distance to which your sketch will be extruded.

    Mid Plane   Mid Plane extrudes your sketch equally in both directions away from the sketch plane to a specified overall depth.

    To Plane   To Plane extrudes the sketch to an existing work plane or planar face.

    Through   The Through method of termination allows the cut or intersection to run through the entire depth of the part. Through is used only for removing material from the model. Even if your model is later extended, the cut still remains through the part.

Size   The last set of options specifies the numeric values of extrusion distance and draft angle.

    Distance   Distance is the actual distance your sketch will be extruded; it is valid only for Blind or Mid Plane termination settings.

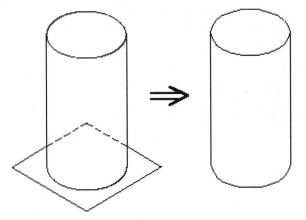

Figure 4-4

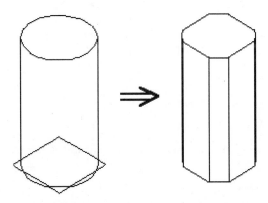

Figure 4-5

Draft Angle   Draft Angle allows you to add either a positive or negative draft angle to your extruded part. With a **positive draft angle,** the profile increases in size as it is extruded away from the sketch plane. A **negative draft angle** produces the opposite result: the profile decreases in size as it is extruded away from the sketch plane. Most molded parts designed for industry require some draft in order to remove the parts from the mold. In a midplane extrusion, draft is added in both directions from the sketch plane. Figure 4–6 shows a profile and the front views that result when this profile is extruded with draft using a midplane extrusion.

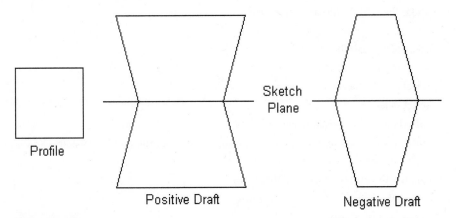

Figure 4-6

The options for the ADEXTRUDE command are fairly basic. Of all the geometric features, you will probably use the extrusion feature more frequently than the other features when you create your solid models.

ADEXTRUDE TUTORIAL

The following tutorial covers a basic extrusion. Your final model should appear as shown in Figure 4–7.

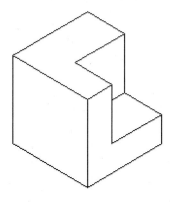

Figure 4-7

1. Start a new drawing in AutoCAD Designer and name it extrude1.

   Command: **new**

   Type **extrude1** in the New Drawing Name edit box.

   Choose **OK.**

2. Create your Scrap, Dimension, Construction, and Model layers as described in Appendix A.

3. Set Scrap as the current layer.

4. Change the **isolines** display setting to four for easier viewing. The visual effect of the isoline display is discussed in detail in Chapter 10.

   Command: **adisolines**

   Isolines for cones, cylinders, and torii<2>: **4**

   Isolines for nurbs<0>: ↵

5. Use AutoCAD's line command to draw a block similar to that shown in Figure 4–8.

6. Make the sketch into an active profile.

   Command: **adprofile**

   Select objects for sketch.

   Select objects: *Select the entire block.*

   Select objects: ↵

   Solved under constrained sketch requiring 2 dimensions/constraints.

   Note: Your message may vary slightly depending on the current system variable settings and the accuracy of your rough sketch.

7. Change the current layer to Dimension.

8. Check the constraints on your profile.

   Command: **adshowcon**

   All/Select/Next/<eXit>: **a**

Figure 4-8

Your profile should contain the constraints shown in Figure 4–9. Add any constraints that are missing.

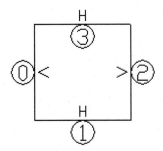

Figure 4-9

9. Create a global parameter to be used for the dimensions of your base cube.

   Command: **adparam**

   Create/Delete/List/Import/Export/<eXit>: **c**

   Enter equation: **cube1=12**

   Parameter "cube1" created: current value == 12

   Enter equation: ↵

10. Dimension your profile.

   Command: **adpardim**

   Select first item: *Pick P1 of Figure 4–10.*

   Select second item or place dimension: *Pick P2.*

   Undo/Hor/Ver/Align/Par/Dimension value<current>: **cube1**

   Solved under constrained sketch requiring 1 dimension/constraint.

   Select first item: *Pick P3.*

   Select second item or place dimension: *Pick P4.*

   Undo/Hor/Ver/Align/Par/Dimension value<current>: **cube1**

   Solved fully constrained sketch.

   Select first item: ↵

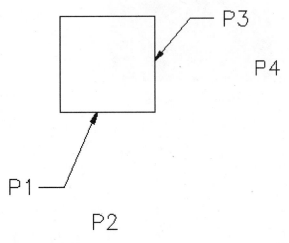

Figure 4-10

11. Switch to an isometric view to view the part as it is extruded. Your dimensioned profile should now look similar to that of Figure 4–11.

Command: **adpartview**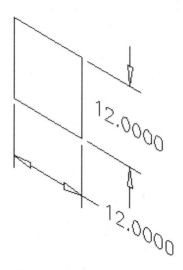

View option Front/Right/Left/Top/Bottom/Isometric/<Sketch>: **I**

Figure 4-11

12. Change the current layer to Model.

13. This is a good point to mark the work you have completed before performing the extrusion. If your extrusion does not turn out the way you want it, you have an immediate reference point to move back to.

    Command: **undo**

    Auto/Back/Control/End/Group/Mark/<number>: **m**

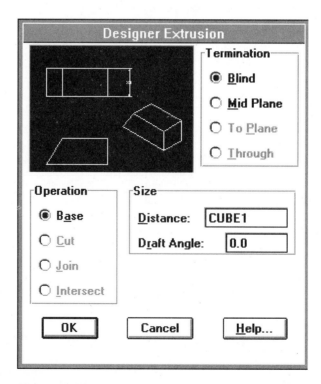

Figure 4-12

14. Extrude the profile using the ADEXTRUDE command.

    Command: **adextrude**

    Set the dialogue box options as shown in Figure 4–12. Select **OK.**

    Your extruded profile should now resemble that of Figure 4–13. Notice that the figure appears similar to a wire-frame part. The features are actually solid models, but unless the parts are meshed and rendered they will appear as shown.

    You can now use the same sketch plane that the base feature was created on to remove a section of the cube.

15. Return the Part view to the Sketch view.

    Command: **adpartview**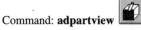

    View Option Front/Right/Left/Top/Bottom/Isometric/<Sketch>: **s**

16. Set Scrap as the current layer.

17. Sketch an additional block inside the previous cube similar to that shown in Figure 4–14.

18. Make the sketch into an active profile and be sure not to select the extruded cube. Notice that this profile needs two more dimensions/constraints than the previous profile required. Unlike the base feature created previously, additional features need to be constrained to existing model geometry.

    Command: **adprofile**

    Select objects for sketch.

    Select objects: *Select the new sketched block.*

    Select objects: ↵

    Solved under constrained sketch requiring 4 dimensions/constraints.

    Note: Your message may vary slightly depending on the current system variable settings and the accuracy of your rough sketch.

19. Change the current layer to Dimension.

20. Check the constraints on your profile.

    Command: **adshowcon**

    All/Select/Next/<eXit>: **a**

    Your profile should contain the constraints shown in Figure 4–15. Add any constraints that are missing.

21. Project the profile off the top-right corner of the previously created cube.

    Command: **adaddcon**

    Hor/Ver/PErp/PAr/Tan/CL/CN/PRoj/Join/XValue/Yvalue/Radius/<eXit>: **cl**

    Select first line: *Select vertical line P1 of Figure 4–16.*

    Select second line: *Select vertical line P2 of the extruded cube.*

    Solved under constrained sketch requiring 3 dimensions/constraints.

    Hor/Ver/PErp/PAr/Tan/CL/CN/PRoj/Join/XValue/Yvalue/Radius/<eXit>: **cl**

    Select first line: *Select horizontal line P3.*

    Select second line: *Select horizontal line P4 of the extruded cube.*

    Solved under constrained sketch requiring 2 dimensions/constraints.

22. Finish constraining the profile with dimensions.

    Command: **adpardim**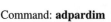

    Select first item: *Pick P1 of Figure 4–17.*

    Select second item or place dimension: *Pick P2.*

    Undo/Hor/Ver/Align/Par/Dimension value<current>: **=cube1/2**

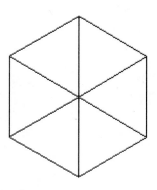

Figure 4-13

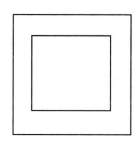

Figure 4-14

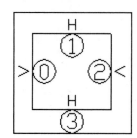

Figure 4-15

Solved under constrained sketch requiring 1 dimension/constraint.

Select first item: *Pick P3.*

Select second item or place dimension: *Pick P4.*

Undo/Hor/Ver/Align/Par/Dimension value<current>: **=cube1/2+2**⏎

Solved fully constrained sketch.

Select first item: ⏎

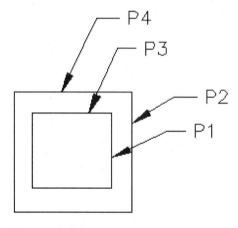

Figure 4-16

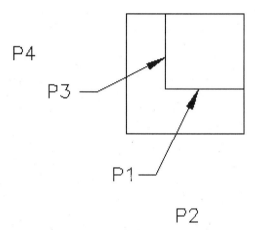

Figure 4-17

23. Switch to an isometric view to view the part as it is extruded. Your dimensioned profile should now look similar to that of Figure 4–18.

    Command: **adpartview**

    View option Front/Right/Left/Top/Bottom/Isometric/<Sketch>: **I**

24. Change the current layer to Model.

25. Once again, this is a good point to mark the work you have completed before performing the extrusion. Remember, this has been a simple part to constrain. It is good practice to use undo marks between dimensioning steps when you get into more complicated geometry.

    Command: **undo**

    Auto/Back/Control/End/Group/Mark/<number>: **m**

26. Extrude the profile using the ADEXTRUDE command, this time cutting material away from the base part.

    Command: **adextrude**

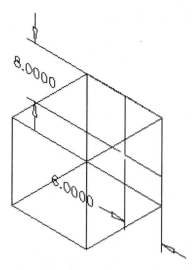

Figure 4-18

Set the dialogue box options as shown in Figure 4–19. Select **OK**.

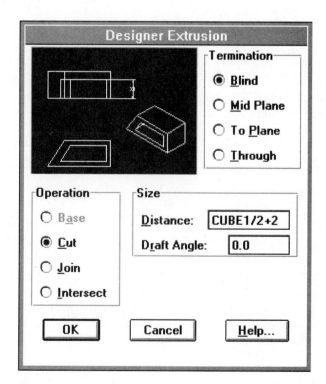

Figure 4-19

Finally, your extruded profile should now resemble that of Figure 4–20. Save your work.

ADSKPLN

ADSKPLN allows you to set the current location of the sketch plane along with the XY orientation. A sketch plane is an infinite plane in space on which you intend to sketch the next profile or path.

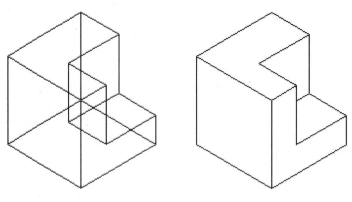

Figure 4-20

Command: **adskpln**

Xy/Yz/Zx/Ucs/<Select work plane or planar face>: *Choose a work plane or planar face or select an option.*

X/Y/Z/<Select work axis or straight edge>: *Choose a work axis or straight edge or select an option.*

Rotate/<Accept>: *Accept the current User Coordinate System orientation or select Rotate to display a different orientation.*

The Xy, Yz, and Zx options as well as the X, Y, and Z options refer to the World Coordinate System. When you begin a new drawing, the sketch plane is automatically the WCS XY plane. If you wish to begin with a different sketch plane, such as WCS YZ or WCS XZ, use the ADSKPLN command and select a different sketch plane. If you set the **User Coordinate System** (UCS) to an orientation different than the standard WCS, the XY plane of the UCS could also be used to locate a sketch plane.

Helpful Hint: The UCS option for creating a sketch plane is not recommended. This method is non-parametric and cannot be changed as you go back to edit your model.

A work plane is not needed to create a sketch plane. A sketch plane may be defined by a planar surface on your model. Using model surfaces for sketch planes reduces the number of work planes that need to be created, thereby making it easier to view the various features of your drawing. Work planes do need to be used where model surfaces do not exist; work planes are discussed later in this chapter.

ADSKPLN TUTORIAL

This lesson not only demonstrates the use of the ADSKPLN command but also reviews the use of the ADEXTRUDE command to create three-dimensional solid extruded parts. The completed model created with this tutorial is the block shown in Figure 4–21. Before beginning this exercise, consider the various design options. Ask yourself what is the most efficient route or which route makes the most sense for constraining your part. Since you will be dealing with a fairly simple profile in this example, you can start with the overall shape; then by switching the sketch plane, cut away the hole. Finish the part off by cutting away the section in the middle. In engineering there are always several design options. Make sure you have a full understanding of the part you will be creating and organize your thoughts and procedures before moving ahead.

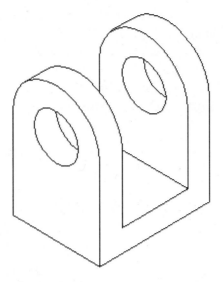

Figure 4-21

1. Start a new drawing in AutoCAD Designer and name it extrude2.

   Command: **new**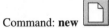

   Type **extrude2** in the New Drawing Name edit box.

   Choose **OK.**

2. Create layers Scrap, Dimension, Construction, and Model as described in Appendix A.

3. Set Scrap as the current layer.

4. Change the isolines display for easier viewing.

   Command: **adisolines**

   Isolines for cones, cylinders, and torii<2>: **4**

   Isolines for nurbs<0>: ↵

5. Use AutoCAD's line and arc commands to draw a shape similar to that shown in Figure 4–22.

6. Make the sketch into a profile.

   Command: **adprofile**

   Select objects for sketch.

   Select objects: *Select the entire block.*

   Select objects: ↵

   Solved under constrained sketch requiring 2 dimensions/constraints.

   Note: Your message may vary slightly.

7. Check the constraints on your profile.

   Command: **adshowcon**

   All/Select/Next/<eXit>: **a**

   Your profile should contain the constraints shown in Figure 4–23. Add any constraints that are missing.

8. Change the current layer to Dimension.

9. Dimension your profile.

   Command: **adpardim**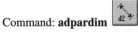

   Select first item: *Pick arc P1 of Figure 4–24.*

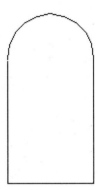

Figure 4-22

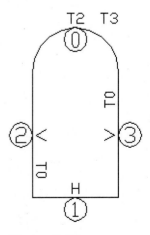

Figure 4-23

Select second item or place dimension: *Pick P2.*

Undo/Hor/Ver/Align/Par/Dimension value<current>: **1**

Solved under constrained sketch requiring 1dimension/constraint.

Select first item: *Pick vertical line P3.*

Select second item or place dimension: *Pick P4.*

Undo/Hor/Ver/Align/Par/Dimension value<current>: **2**

Solved fully constrained sketch.

Select first item: ↵

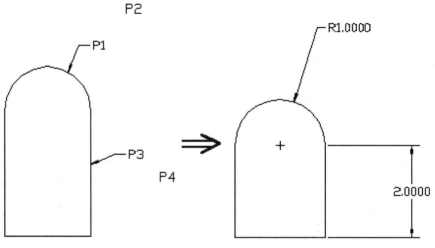

Figure 4-24

10. Switch to an isometric view to view the part as it is extruded. Your dimensioned profile should now look similar to that of Figure 4–25.

Command: **adpartview**

View option Front/Right/Left/Top/Bottom/Isometric/<Sketch>: **i**

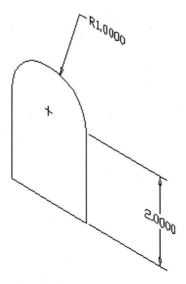

Figure 4-25

11. This is a good point to mark the work you have completed before performing the extrusion. If your extrusion does not turn out the way you want it, you have an immediate reference point to move back to.

Command: **undo**

Auto/Back/Control/End/Group/Mark/<number>: **m**

12. Change the current layer to Model.

13. Use the ADEXTRUDE command to extrude the part.

Command: **adextrude**

Set the dialogue box options as shown in Figure 4–26. Select **OK.**

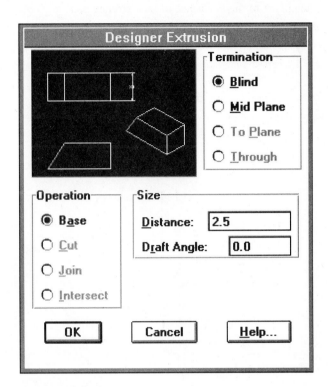

Figure 4-26

Your extruded profile should now resemble that of Figure 4–27.

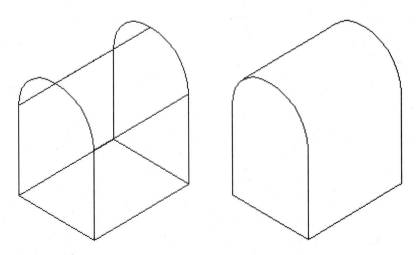

Figure 4-27

Now that you have the solid block, the next feature to create is the extruded hole through the part. In Chapter 7 you will learn the ADHOLE feature command, but for now you can practice the ADEXTRUDE command. In the design stage of this particular part, it does not matter whether the block or the hole is cut out first because both options require the same number of operations.

Currently, the sketch plane is located on the back side of the extruded block. This sketch plane could be used to locate the circle profile, but because you need to practice creating sketch planes, you will move its location to the front side of the extruded part. In addition, you will try using the AutoCAD VPORTS command so that you can look at both the Sketch view and the Isometric view at the same time.

14. Move the sketch plane to the front face of the extruded part.

   Command: **adskpln**

   Xy/Yz/Zx/Ucs/<Select work plane or planar face>: *Pick P1 of Figure 4–28.*

   Next/<Accept>: *Select next until your plane matches the highlighted plane shown in Figure 4–28; then accept.*

   X/Y/Z/<Select work axis or straight edge>: **x**↵

   Rotate/<Accept>: ↵

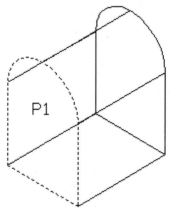

Figure 4–28

15. Set the viewports to show both the Sketch view and the Isometric view of the model.

   Command: **vports**

   Save/Restore/Delete/Join/SIngle/?/2/<3>/4: **2**

   Horizontal/<Vertical>: **vertical**

   The screen should now show two identical isometric views as shown in Figure 4–29.

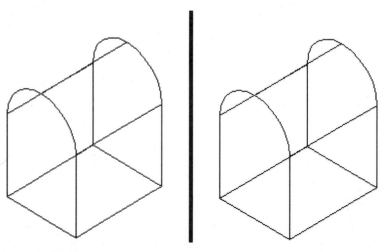

Figure 4–29

Click on the left viewport to make it active and switch to Sketch view.

Command: **adpartview**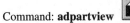

View option Front/Right/Left/Top/Bottom/Isometric/<Sketch>: **s**

Now anything drawn on the Sketch view will also be displayed on the Isometric view.

16. Switch the current layer to Scrap.

17. Draw a circle on the sketch plane, as shown in Figure 4–30.

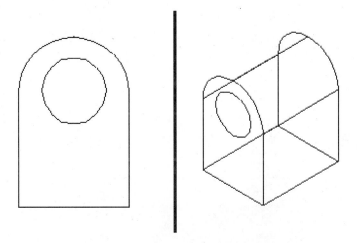

Figure 4–30

18. Make the circle an active profile.

Command: **adprofile**

Select objects for sketch.

Select objects: *Select the circle.*

Select objects: ↵

Solved under constrained sketch requiring 3 dimensions/constraints.

19. Switch layers again to activate the Dimension layer. Constrain the sketch to your model.

Command: **adpardim**

Select first item: *Pick circle P1 of Figure 4–31.*

Select second item or place dimension: *Pick P2.*

Undo/Hor/Ver/Align/Par/Dimension value<current>: **1**

Solved under constrained sketch requiring 2 dimensions/constraints.

Select first item: ↵

Command: **adaddcon**

Hor/Ver/PErp/PAr/Tan/CL/CN/Proj/Join/XValue/Yvalue/Radius/<eXit>: **cn**

Select first arc or circle: *Pick circle P1.*

Select second arc or circle: *Pick arc P3.*

Solved fully constrained sketch.

Hor/Ver/PErp/PAr/Tan/CL/CN/Proj/Join/XValue/Yvalue/Radius/<eXit>: ↵

20. Mark this point and extrude the hole through your model.

Command: **undo**

Auto/Back/Control/End/Group/Mark/<number>: **m**

Command: **adextrude**

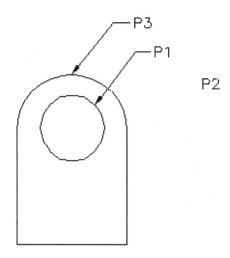

Figure 4-31

Set the dialogue box options as shown in Figure 4–32. Select **OK**.

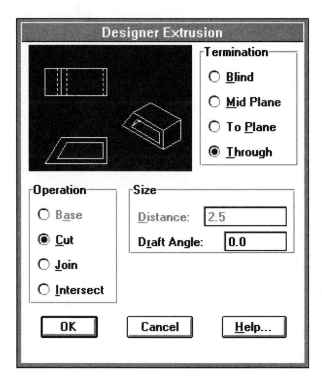

Figure 4-32

Flip the direction of the extrusion only if the arrow is pointing away from your block; otherwise, accept.

Flip/<Accept>: ↵

Your isometric block should now look like that of Figure 4–33.

21. Now that you have cut your hole out from your part, the next logical step is to remove the block from the middle in a similar manner. Start by clicking on the Isometric view so you can change the active sketch plane to the adjacent side.

Command: **adskpln**

Xy/Yz/Zx/Ucs/<Select work plane or planar face>: *Pick P1 of Figure 4–34.*

Next/<Accept>: *Select next until your plane matches the highlighted plane shown in Figure 4–34 and then accept.*

X/Y/Z/<Select work axis or straight edge>: **y**

Rotate/<Accept>: *Rotate until your axis is orientated as shown in Figure 4–34 and then accept.*

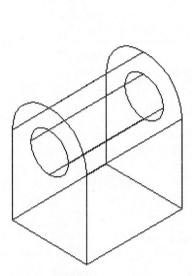

Figure 4–33

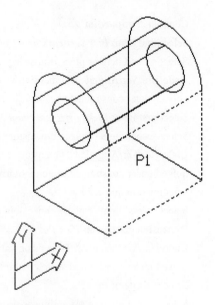

Figure 4–34

22. Set Scrap as the current layer.

23. With the isometric viewport current, draw a rectangle inside your block similar to that of Figure 4–35.

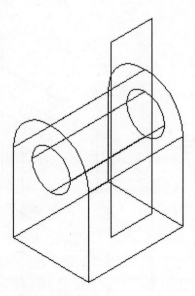

Figure 4–35

24. Make the sketch into a profile.

Command: **adprofile**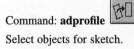

Select objects for sketch.

Select objects: *Select the rectangle created.*

Select objects: ↵

Solved under constrained sketch requiring 4 dimensions/constraints.

25. Switch back to the Dimension layer and begin constraining your profile to the model.

Command: **adpardim**

Select first item: *Pick vertical line P1 of Figure 4–36.*

Select second item or place dimension: *Pick P2.*

Undo/Hor/Ver/Align/Par/Dimension value<current>: **2.5**

Solved under constrained sketch requiring 3 dimensions/constraints.

Select first item: *Pick horizontal line P3.*

Select second item or place dimension: *Pick P4.*

Undo/Hor/Ver/Align/Par/Dimension value<current>: **1.5**

Solved under constrained sketch requiring 2 dimensions/constraints.

Select first item: *Pick P1.*

Select second item or place dimension: *Pick P5.*

Dimension placement: *Pick P6.*

Undo/Hor/Ver/Align/Par/Dimension value<current>: **0.5**

Solved under constrained sketch requiring 1 dimension/constraint.

Select first item: *Pick P1.*

Select second item or place dimension: *Pick P5.*

Dimension placement: *Pick P7.*

Undo/Hor/Ver/Align/Par/Dimension value<current>: **0.5**

Solved fully constrained sketch.

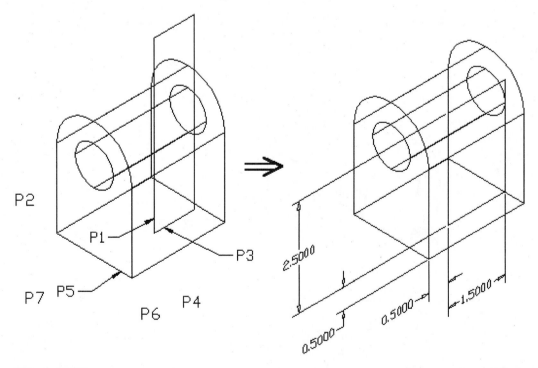

Figure 4–36

26. Mark this point and cut out the block from your model.

Command: **undo**

Auto/Back/Control/End/Group/Mark/<number>: **m**

Command: **adextrude**

Set the dialogue box options as shown in Figure 4–37. Select **OK.**

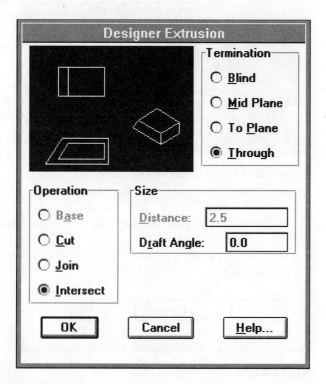

Figure 4-37

Flip the direction of the extrusion arrow only if it is pointing away from your block; otherwise, accept.

Flip/<Accept>: ↵

27. Instead of the part shown in Figure 4–21, you have created the intersection of the extruded profile and the existing model as shown in Figure 4–38.

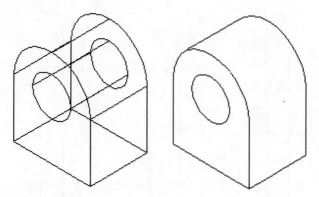

Figure 4-38

28. Return to the point just before the extrusion was made and this time make the extrusion operation a cut rather than an intersection.

Command: **undo**

Auto/Back/Control/End/Group/Mark/<number>: **b**

Command: **adextrude**

Set the dialogue box options as shown in Figure 4–39. Select **OK.**

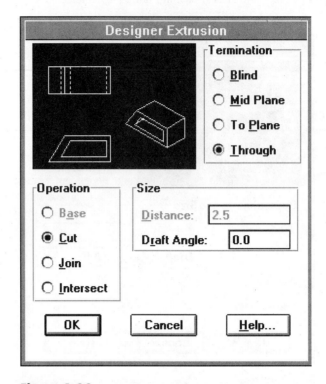

Figure 4-39

Again, choose flip only if your arrow is pointing away from your block.
Flip/<Accept>: ↵
You should now see the original part shown in Figure 4–40.

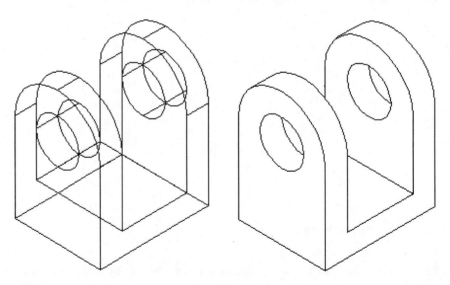

Figure 4-40

29. Be sure to save your work before exiting AutoCAD.

ADWORKPLN

Work planes are important tools that aid in the process of constructing a parametric model. Work planes extend infinitely in either direction in model space, although on screen they appear finite. Work planes can be either parametric or non-parametric, meaning that they may or may not be modified later. Although the planes are attached to your model, they will not plot with your drawing and do not appear in any orthographic views when created. Work planes are not three-dimensional entities and therefore do not add any volume to the model's mass properties.

Note: AutoCAD Designer places all work features such as planes, axes, and points, on the ADP_WORK layer. Never work on the ADP_WORK layer. Altering its contents may permanently corrupt your database.

There are 12 options for parametric work planes and four for non-parametric work planes. If a parametric work plane is modified, any dependent features are modified accordingly; however, non-parametric work planes will not cause a model update if they are modified. For this reason, the use of non-parametric work planes is not recommended.

Work planes have many uses, such as defining sketch planes, defining feature placements and terminations, and defining section planes when working with orthographic views. Work planes are created using the ADWORKPLN command. The Designer Work Plane dialogue box displays all the available options for the ADWORKPLN command. See Figure 4–41. Many of these options open a second dialogue box. The second option is needed to fully constrain the work plane. Most of the option combinations are repeated; however, the order in which you choose the options makes no difference to their operation.

Command: **adworkpln**

Figure 4-41

The various work plane options are described next.

On Edge/Axis // On Edge/Axis   Work plane is defined by two edges of a model, two work axes, or a model edge and a work axis. See Figure 4–42.

Practical Application: Use to locate a work plane that passes through the centers of two cylindrical objects. The Work plane will be used later as a section cutting plane for drawing views.

On Edge/Axis // On Vertex   Work plane is defined by a model edge or a work axis along with a vertex point. See Figure 4–43.

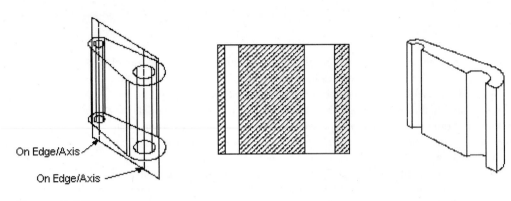

Figure 4-42

Practical Application: Use to define a work plane for creating slanted slots, etc.

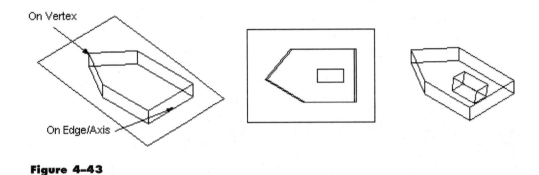

Figure 4-43

On Edge/Axis // Tangent   Work plane is defined by a model edge or a work axis along with a cylinder from which a tangency is to be applied. See Figure 4–44.

Practical Application: Use for creating a hole perpendicular to another cylinder whose center is tangent as specified by the work plane.

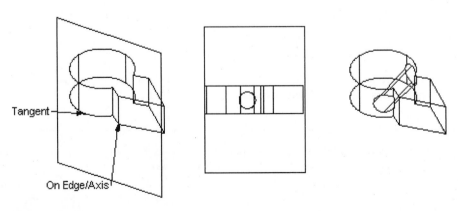

Figure 4-44

On Edge/Axis // Planar Parallel   Work plane is defined by a model edge or a work axis along with a defined plane. See Figure 4–45.

Practical Application: An edge or axis is a common offset from an existing work plane or planar face. This is the most popular option combination for the creation of a work plane.

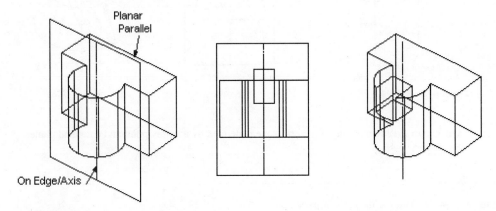

Figure 4–45

On Edge/Axis // Planar Normal   Work plane is defined by a model edge or a work axis along with a defined plane. See Figure 4–46.

Note: Sometimes this option combination results in multiple possible solutions. If this is the case, AutoCAD Designer states "Cannot construct valid work plane. Could not construct feature."

Practical Application: Use to create perpendicular work planes for feature creations.

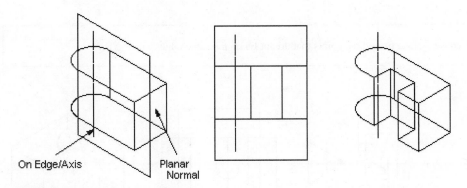

Figure 4–46

On Edge/Axis // Planar Angle   Work plane is defined by a model edge or a work axis, a defined plane, and an angle. Two possible solutions always exist depending on the direction of the angle. You can change the direction of the angle by flipping it and then accepting the angle when it is toward the intended direction. See Figure 4–47.

Practical Application: Use to create work planes by a known angular difference, which otherwise might be difficult to create parametrically.

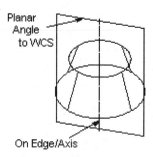 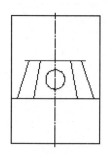 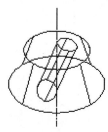

Figure 4-47

On Vertex // Planar Parallel   Work plane is defined by a vertex point and a defined plane. See Figure 4–48.

Practical Application: Use to create work planes at the apex of pyramids.

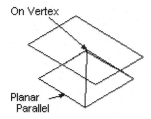 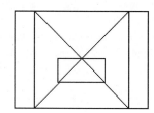 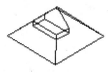

Figure 4-48

On Vertex // 3 Vertices   Work plane is defined by three vertex points. See Figure 4–49.

Practical Application: Use to create a plane from three points that do not lie on the same edge/axis.

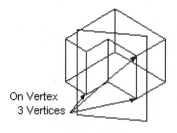 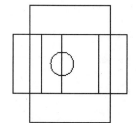 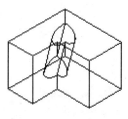

Figure 4-49

Tangent // Planar Parallel   Work plane is determined by a defined plane and a cylinder from which a tangency can be applied. See Figure 4–50.

Practical Application: Use as a sketch plane for extrusions.

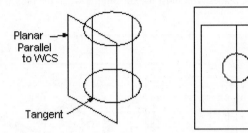
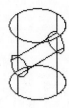

Figure 4–50

Tangent // Planar Normal   Work plane is determined by the **normal** from a defined plane and a cylinder from which tangency can be applied. See Figure 4–51.

Note: Sometimes more than one solution can exist from these options. If this happens, AutoCAD Designer will state "Cannot construct valid work plane. Could not construct feature."

Practical Application: Use as a sketch plane for extrusions.

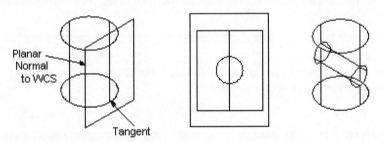

Figure 4–51

Sweep Plane   Work plane is automatically created normal to a sweep path at its start point. See Figure 4–52.

Practical Application: This option must be used for all sweeps.

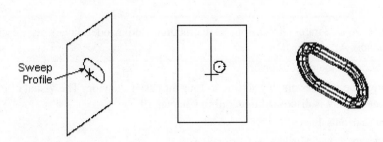

Figure 4–52

Planar Parallel // Offset   Work plane is determined by a defined plane and a specified offset distance. See Figure 4–53.

Practical Application: This is a very useful method for creating work planes. You must use this option when the only information you know is the offset distance.

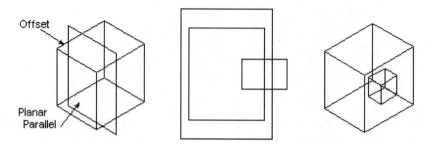

Figure 4-53

Non-Parametric Work Planes   Non-parametric work planes are defined by the UCS or the WCS.

Practical Application: Although at times it may seem faster and easier to create a work plane directly on a UCS or a WCS, this practice is not recommended. Non-parametric work planes will never update with your model; once created they stay put. Use non-parametric work planes only as a last resort.

Create Sketch Plane   The Create Sketch Plane option allows you to make the newly created work plane into the current sketch plane.

ADWORKPLN TUTORIAL

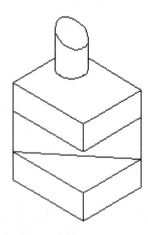

Like the previous tutorials in this chapter, this tutorial incorporates the ADEXTRUDE feature command. A majority of the work planes you create are likely to be used as sketch planes for creating an extrusion. This tutorial uses a typical sketch plane example and also gives a unique example of how a work plane can help in creating model features. Your final model should appear as shown in Figure 4–54.

1. Start a new drawing in AutoCAD Designer and name it extrude3.

   Command: **new**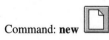

   Type **extrude3** in the New Drawing Name edit box.

   Choose **OK.**

2. Create your Scrap, Dimension, Construction, and Model layers as described in Appendix A.

Figure 4-54

3. Set Scrap as the current layer.

4. Change the isolines display setting to four for easier viewing. The visual effect of the isoline display is discussed in detail in Chapter 10.

   Command: **adisolines**

   Isolines for cones, cylinders, and torii<2>: **4**

   Isolines for nurbs<0>: ↵

5. Draw a block similar to that shown in Figure 4–55.

Figure 4-55

6. Make the sketch into an active profile.

Command: **adprofile**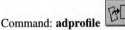

Select objects for sketch.

Select objects: *Select the entire block.*

Select objects: ↵

Solved under constrained sketch requiring 2 dimensions/constraints.

Note: Your message may vary slightly depending on the current system variable settings and the accuracy of your rough sketch.

7. Change the current layer to Dimension.

8. Check the constraints on your profile.

Command: **adshowcon**

All/Select/Next/<eXit>: **a**

Your profile should contain the constraints shown in Figure 4–56. Add any constraints that are missing.

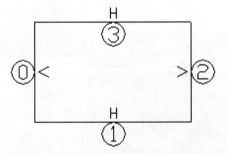

Figure 4-56

9. Dimension your profile.

Command: **adpardim**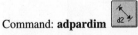

Select first item: *Pick P1 of Figure 4–57.*

Select second item or place dimension: *Pick P2.*

Undo/Hor/Ver/Align/Par/Dimension value<current>: **7**

Solved under constrained sketch requiring 1 dimension/constraint.

Select first item: *Pick P3.*

Select second item or place dimension: *Pick P4.*

Undo/Hor/Ver/Align/Par/Dimension value<current>: **6**

Solved fully constrained sketch.

Select first item: ↵

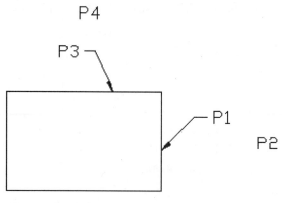

Figure 4–57

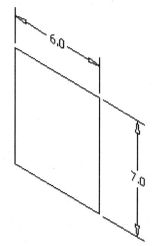

Figure 4–58

10. Switch to an isometric view to view the part as it is extruded. Your dimensioned profile should now look similar to that of Figure 4–58.

Command: **adpartview**

View option Front/Right/Left/Top/Bottom/Isometric/<Sketch>: **i**

11. Change the current layer to Model.

12. This is a good point to mark the work you have completed before performing the extrusion. If your extrusion does not turn out the way you want it, you have an immediate reference point to move back to.

Command: **undo**

Auto/Back/Control/End/Group/Mark/<number>: **m**

13. Use the ADEXTRUDE command to extrude the profile.

Command: **adextrude**

Set the dialogue box options as shown in Figure 4–59. Select **OK.**

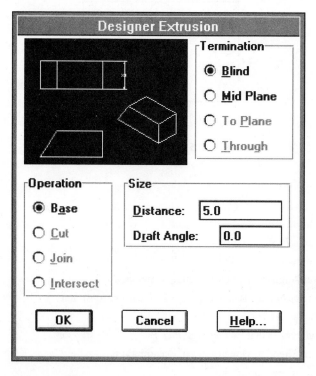

Figure 4–59

Your extruded profile should now resemble that of Figure 4–60.

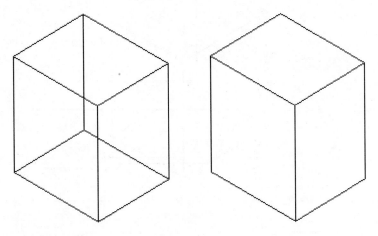

Figure 4–60

14. You are now ready to add a work plane across a diagonal of your base feature. In the dialogue boxes shown in Figure 4–61, select the On Edge/Axis // On Edge/Axis combination and also mark the box to make the work plane the active sketch plane.

    Command: **adworkpln**

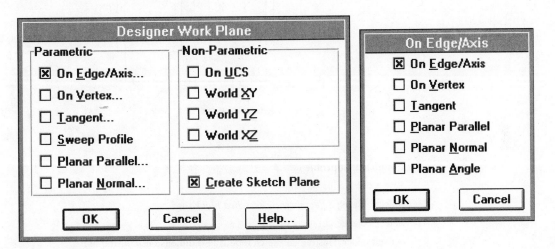

Figure 4–61

X/Y/Z/<Select work axis or straight edge>: *Select edge P1 of Figure 4–62.*

X/Y/Z/<Select work axis or straight edge>: *Select edge P2.*

X/Y/Z/<Select work axis or straight edge>: **x**

Rotate/<Accept>: ↵

15. Switch to the newly created Sketch view.

    Command: **adpartview**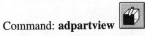

    View option Front/Right/Left/Top/Bottom/Isometric/<Sketch>: **s**

16. Set Scrap as the current layer.

17. Draw a rectangle in the middle of your sketch plane as shown in Figure 4–63.

18. Make the sketch into an active profile and be sure not to select the extruded block.

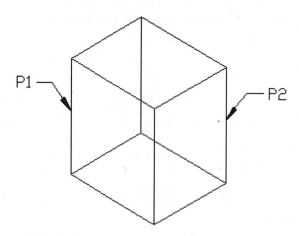

Figure 4–62

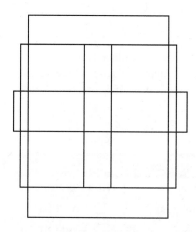

Figure 4–63

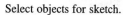

Command: **adprofile**

Select objects for sketch.

Select objects: *Select the new sketched block.*

Select objects: ↵

Solved under constrained sketch requiring 4 dimensions/constraints.

Note: Your message may vary slightly depending on the current system variable settings and the accuracy of your rough sketch.

19. Change the current layer to Dimension.

20. Check the constraints on your profile.

Command: **adshowcon**

All/Select/Next/<eXit>: **a**

Your profile should contain the constraints shown in Figure 4–64. Add any constraints that are missing.

21. Use collinear constraints so that the lines of your new rectangle line up with the edges of your model.

Command: **adaddcon**

Hor/Ver/PErp/PAr/Tan/CL/CN/PRoj/Join/XValue/Yvalue/Radius/<eXit>: **cl**

Select first line: *Pick vertical line P1 of Figure 4–65.*

Select second line: *Select edge P2.*

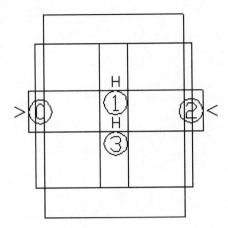

Figure 4–64

Solved under constrained sketch requiring 3 dimensions/constraints.
Hor/Ver/PErp/PAr/Tan/CL/CN/PRoj/Join/XValue/Yvalue/Radius/<eXit>: **cl**
Select first line: *Pick vertical line P3.*
Select second line: *Select edge P4.*
Solved under constrained sketch requiring 2 dimensions/constraints.
Hor/Ver/PErp/PAr/Tan/CL/CN/PRoj/Join/XValue/Yvalue/Radius/<eXit>: ↵

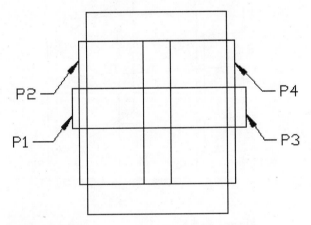

Figure 4–65

22. Now add the dimensional constraints needed to fully constrain your profile.

Command: **adpardim**
Select first item: *Select end of horizontal line P1 of Figure 4–66.*
Select second item or place dimension: *Select end of horizontal line P2.*
Specify dimension placement: *Pick P3.*
Undo/Hor/Ver/Align/Par/Dimension value <current>: **2**
Solved under constrained sketch requiring 1 dimension/constraint.
Select first item: *Select end of horizontal line P4.*
Select second item or place dimension: *Select end of horizontal line P5.*
Specify dimension placement: *Select P6.*
Undo/Hor/Ver/Align/Par/Dimension value <current>: **2**
Solved fully constrained sketch.
Select first item: ↵

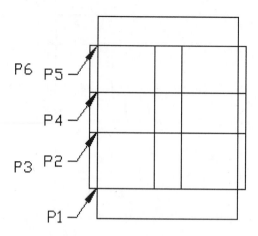

Figure 4-66

23. Switch to an isometric view to view the part as it is extruded. Your dimensioned profile should now look similar to that of Figure 4–67.

Command: **adpartview**

View option Front/Right/Left/Top/Bottom/Isometric/<Sketch>: **i**

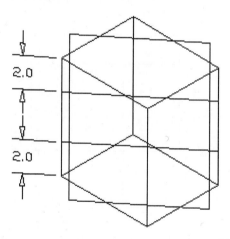

Figure 4-67

24. Change the current layer to Model.

25. Once again, this is a good point to mark the work you have completed before performing the extrusion.

Command: **undo**

Auto/Back/Control/End/Group/Mark/<number>: **m**

26. Use the ADEXTRUDE command to extrude the profile, this time cutting material away from the base part.

Command: **adextrude**

Set the dialogue box options as shown in Figure 4–68. Select **OK.**

Flip the direction of the extrusion arrow if it is pointing toward the back corner of the part.

Flip/<Accept>: *Choose the option necessary.*

Your extruded profile should now resemble that of Figure 4–69. Save your work at this point.

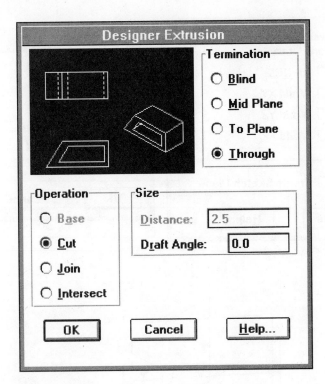

Figure 4-68

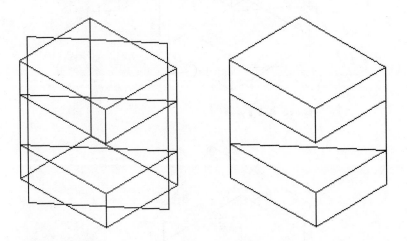

Figure 4-69

27. You now need to add another work plane, but do not make this work plane the active sketch plane. Instead, this will be the surface you are extruding to. With the work plane placed at an angle, the end result is a cylinder with an angled cut off that could not be created without a work plane. In the dialogue boxes shown in Figure 4–70, select the On Edge/Axis // Planar Angle combination.

Command: **adworkpln**

X/Y/Z/<Select work axis or straight edge>: *Select edge P1 of Figure 4–71.*

Xy/Yz/Zx/Ucs/<Select work plane or planar face>: **z**

Angle in degrees <45>: **30**

Flip until the UCS is oriented as shown in Figure 4–72.

Flip/<Accept>: **f**

Flip/<Accept>: ↵

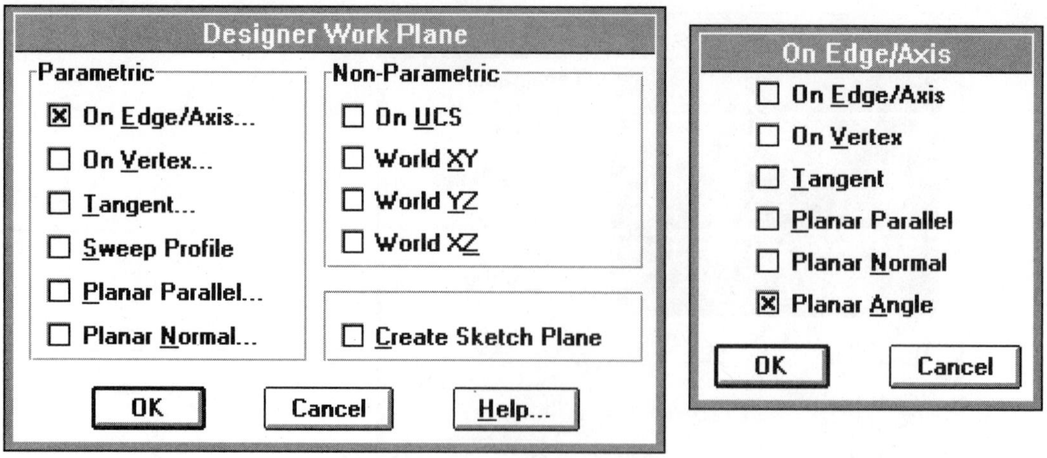

Figure 4-70

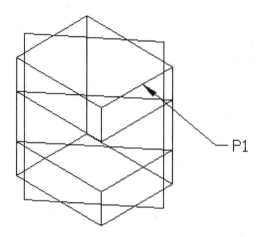

Figure 4-71

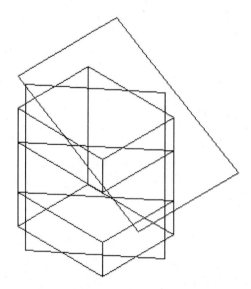

Figure 4-72

28. Make the top face of your model the active sketch plane.

    Command: **adskpln**

    Xy/Yz/Zx/Ucs/<Select work plane or planar face>: *Select top planar face P1 of Figure 4–73.*

Next/<Accept>: ↵

X/Y/Z/<Select work axis or straight edge>: **x**

Rotate/<Accept>: ↵

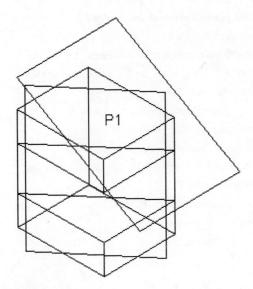

Figure 4-73

29. Switch to the newly created Sketch view.

Command: **adpartview**

View option Front/Right/Left/Top/Bottom/Isometric/<Sketch>: **s**

30. Set Scrap as the current layer.

31. Draw a circle in the corner of the part as shown in Figure 4–74.

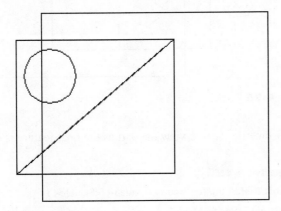

Figure 4-74

32. Make the circle into a profile.

Command: **adprofile**

Select objects for sketch.

Select objects: *Pick the circle.*

Select objects: ↵

Solved under constrained sketch requiring 3 dimensions/constraints.

33. Constrain the sketch to the model.

    Command: **adpardim**

    Select first item: *Pick the circle P1 of Figure 4–75.*

    Select second item or place dimension: *Select edge P2.*

    Specify dimension placement: *Pick P3.*

    Undo/Hor/Ver/Align/Par/Dimension value <current>: **1.5**

    Solved under constrained sketch requiring 2 dimensions/constraints.

    Select first item: *Pick the circle P1.*

    Select second item or place dimension: *Select edge P4.*

    Specify dimension placement: *Pick P5.*

    Undo/Hor/Ver/Align/Par/Dimension value <current>: **1.5**

    Solved under constrained sketch requiring 1 dimension/constraint.

    Select first item: *Pick the circle P1.*

    Select second item or place dimension: *Pick P6.*

    Undo/Dimension value <current>: **2**

    Solved fully constrained sketch.

    Select first item: ↵

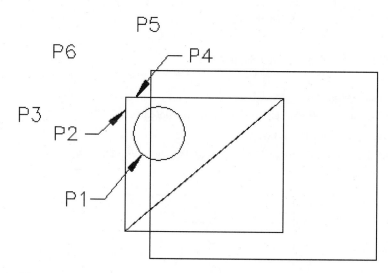

Figure 4–75

34. Switch to an isometric view to view the part as the final feature is extruded.

    Command: **adpartview**

    View option Front/Right/Left/Top/Bottom/Isometric/<Sketch>: **i**

35. Change the current layer to Model.

36. Once again, this is a good point to mark the work you have completed before performing the extrusion.

    Command: **undo**

    Auto/Back/Control/End/Group/Mark/<number>: **m**

37. Use the ADEXTRUDE command to extrude the profile. Rather than a typical cylinder extrusion, the new feature should be cut off at an angle.

    Command: **adextrude**

    Set the dialogue box options as shown in Figure 4–76. Select **OK.**

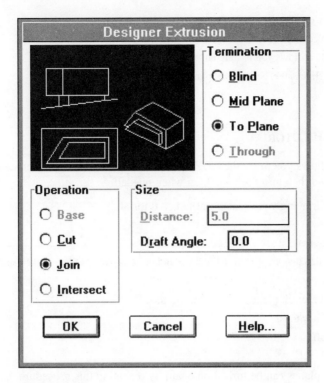

Figure 4-76

Xy/Yz/Zx/Ucs/<Select work plane or planar face>: *Choose the angled work plane.*

38. Finally, your extruded profile should now resemble that of Figure 4–77. Save your work.

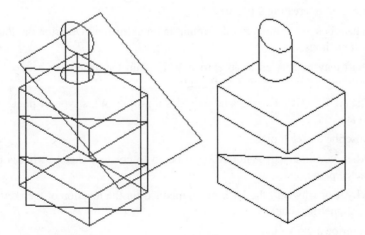

Figure 4-77

ADPLNDSP

ADPLNDSP toggles the display of work planes. If ADPLNDSP is turned on, the planes will be displayed. In order to edit an existing work plane, ADPLNDSP needs to be set to ON.

Command: **adplndsp**

ON/OFF: *Select an option.*

ON   Turns on all work planes.

OFF   Select/<All>: *Select an option.*

Select   Allows you to hide only the work planes that you select.

All   Hides all existing work planes.

ADPLNDSP TUTORIAL

This tutorial allows you to try the ADPLNDSP command to see that you can turn off your work planes and then turn them back on when needed.

1.   Open the drawing you created in the last tutorial.

Command: **open**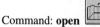

Open extrude3.dwg by selecting the drive and directory of the file and then selecting the file.

Choose **OK.**

2.   Turn off the work planes created in the model.

Command: **adplndsp**

ON/OFF: **off**

Select/<All>: ⏎

The work planes can be turned on again by repeating this procedure, but instead type **on** at the ON/OFF prompt.

REVIEW QUESTIONS

4.1   Name the four different operations of the ADEXTRUDE command. How is each one used in creating a feature?

4.2   What does the termination determine in an extrusion? Describe the four termination methods.

4.3   Draft may be applied to an extrusion. Explain the difference between a positive draft angle and a negative draft angle.

4.4   The ADEXTRUDE command extrudes a profile. What type of plane is a profile created on?

4.5   Describe a sketch plane.

4.6   When you first start AutoCAD and begin to create a sketch, what is the default sketch plane set to?

4.7   Why is or why isn't the UCS recommended for the location of the sketch plane in a parametric model?

4.8   Describe a work plane.

4.9   List all of the parametric combinations that can be used to define the location of a work plane.

4.10   Of the parametric combinations used to define a work plane, which is most effective for placing a work plane two inches from the front face of an extruded block?

CHAPTER EXERCISES

4.1–4.12   From the isometric drawings provided, use extrusion techniques to create the equivalent features. Your final part will look slightly different because the hidden lines will not be removed.

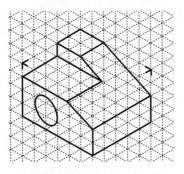

Figure Exer4-1

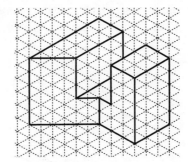

Figure Exer4-2

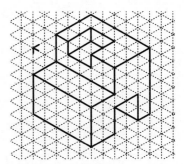

Figure Exer4-3

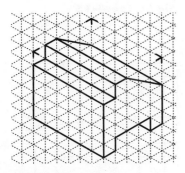

Figure Exer4-4

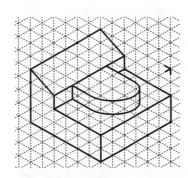

Figure Exer4-5

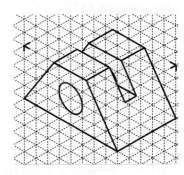

Figure Exer4-6

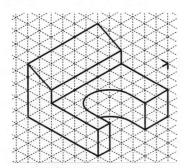

Figure Exer4-7

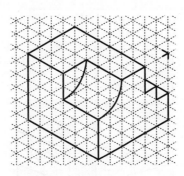

Figure Exer4-8

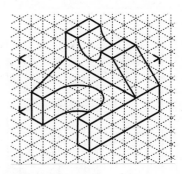

Figure Exer4-9

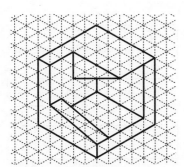

Figure Exer4-10

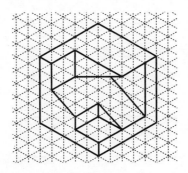

Figure Exer4-11

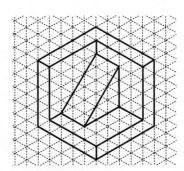

Figure Exer4-12

4.13–4.24   From the orthographic views provided, use extrusion techniques to create the equivalent three-dimensional features.

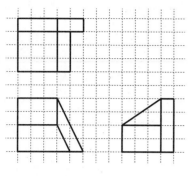

Figure Exer4–13

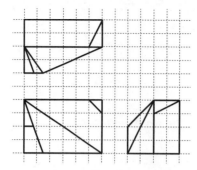

Figure Exer4–14

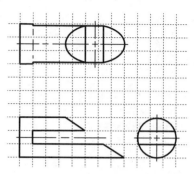

Figure Exer4–15

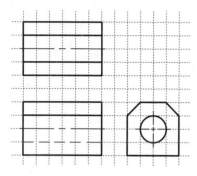

Figure Exer4–16

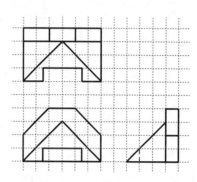

Figure Exer4–17

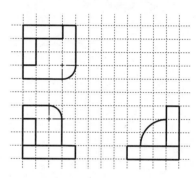

Figure Exer4–18

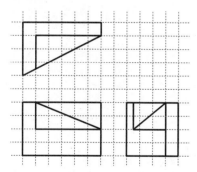

Figure Exer4–19

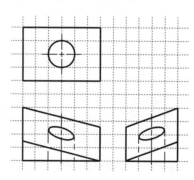

Figure Exer4–20

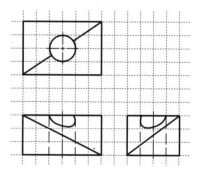

Figure Exer4–21

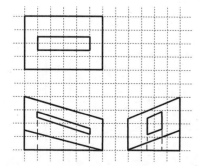

Figure Exer4–22

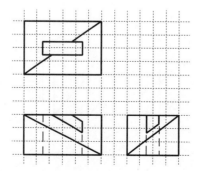

Figure Exer4–23

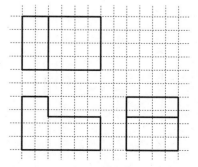

Figure Exer4–24

4.25   From the fully dimensioned isometric drawing, use extrusion techniques to create the retainer clip in Figure Exer4–25.

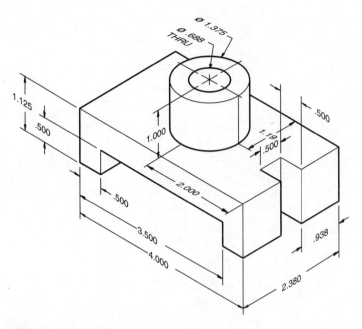

Figure Exer4–25

4.26   From the fully dimensioned isometric drawing, use extrusion techniques to create the slide base in Figure Exer4–26.

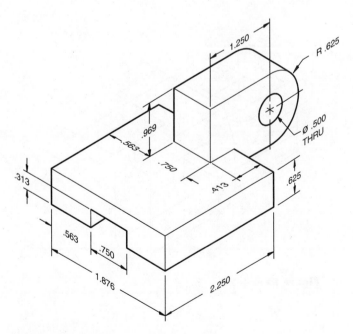

Figure Exer4–26

4.27   From the fully dimensioned isometric drawing, use extrusion techniques to create the strike arm in Figure Exer4–27.

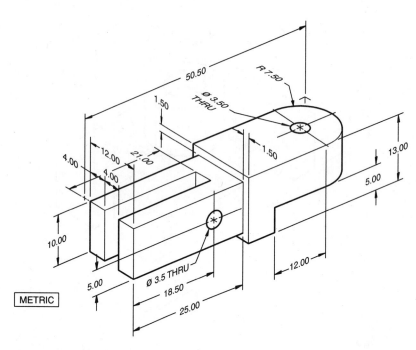

Figure Exer4-27

4.28   From the fully dimensioned isometric drawing, use extrusion techniques to create the tool holder in Figure Exer4–28.

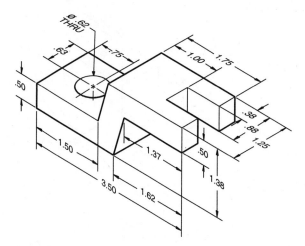

Figure Exer4-28

4.29   From the fully dimensioned isometric drawing, use extrusion techniques to create the dial bracket in Figure Exer4–29.

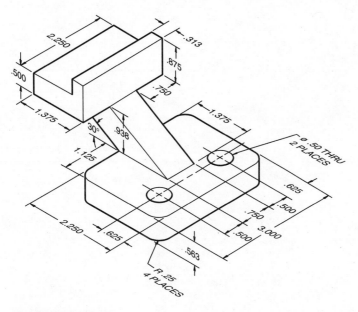

Figure Exer4-29

4.30   From the fully dimensioned isometric drawing, use extrusion techniques to create the pulley support in Figure Exer4–30.

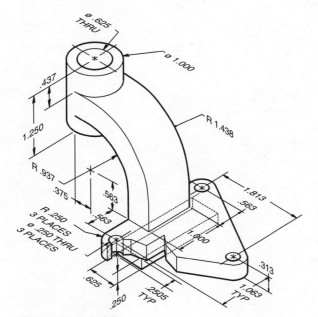

Figure Exer4-30

5

REVOLUTIONS AND AXES

This chapter examines the revolve feature that takes a two-dimensional profile and rotates it about an axis to create a three-dimensional revolved feature. In addition, we will look at the **work axis**, which can be used to rotate a profile around or as an aid in locating a work plane.

ADREVOLVE

The ADREVOLVE command is similar to ADEXTRUDE. Both commands can create a solid feature or remove material from an existing part in a two-dimensional sketch. The obvious difference between the commands is in the way they form three-dimensional features. Remember that the ADEXTRUDE command extends the two-dimensional sketch to a set depth parallel to the sketch plane. ADREVOLVE, however, uses an axis of rotation to revolve the two-dimensional sketch around, thereby creating or cutting away from a solid feature.

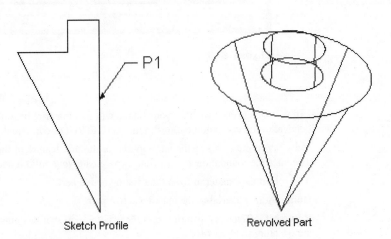

Sketch Profile   Revolved Part

Figure 5–1

Command: **adrevolve**

Select axis of revolution: *Select the axis to be revolved around. P1 in Figure 5–1.*

The following are valid axes for rotation.

• A work axis.

• A straight line edge of a model.

- A straight line of the sketch profile. In addition to being able to use a straight line edge of the profile, a construction line can be offset a specific distance in order to create a hollow or open solid feature. This construction line needs to be a different line type than your profile (centerlines or dashed hidden lines work well) so that AutoCAD Designer can recognize that this line is only an axis and not part of the sketch.

After you choose your axis of revolution, the Designer Revolution dialogue box shown in Figure 5–2 appears.

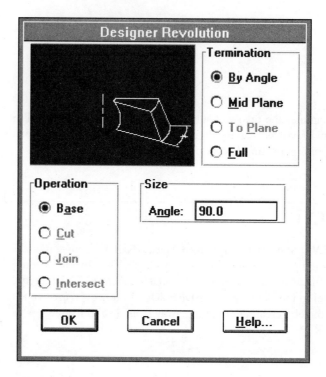

Figure 5-2

Operation   Determines whether your sketch will add material or remove it. These options are identical to the Operation options in the ADEXTRUDE command.

    Base   You must choose the base option for the first feature of the part. A base feature becomes the foundation around which you create your solid model.

    Cut   Removes material from the existing active part.

    Join   Adds material to the existing active part.

    Intersect   Removes material from the existing part that lies outside the volume of the new feature to be revolved.

Termination   Determines the angular position that the sketch will be revolved to. Again, these options are very similar to those described previously for the ADEXTRUDE command.

    By Angle   Allows you to set an angle to which your sketch will be revolved.

    Mid Plane   Revolves your sketch equally in both directions away from the sketch plane to a specified overall angle.

    To Plane   Revolves the sketch to an existing work plane or planar face.

    Full   Revolves the profile 360 degrees.

Size   Specifies the angle if the sketch is being revolved By Angle or Mid Plane.

    Angle   Specifies the angle of revolution in degrees.

ADREVOLVE TUTORIAL

This tutorial uses the ADREVOLVE command to create a geometric feature that is uniform around an axis. By revolving around a line on your profile, you can create a solid shape such as the bat shown in Figure 5–3. In addition, you can create hollow or tubular shapes by revolving around an axis located in space. Upon completion of this lesson, your revolved bat should be similar to Figure 5–3.

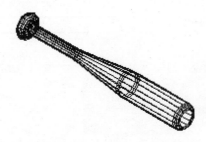

Figure 5-3

1. Start a new drawing in AutoCAD Designer and name it revolve1.

   Command: **new**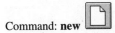

   Type **revolve1** in the New Drawing Name edit box.

   Choose **OK.**

2. Create your AutoCAD Designer layers as described in Appendix A.

3. Set Scrap as the current layer.

4. Change the isolines display for easier viewing. In this lesson, increasing the isolines enables you to visualize the rounded solid shape of the bat.

   Command: **adisolines**

   Isolines for cones, cylinders, and torii<2>: **16**

   Isolines for nurbs<0>: **0**

5. Use line and fillet commands to draw a shape similar to that shown in Figure 5–4. Do not try to make your bat resemble a profile of a normal baseball bat. Create it to be oversized to be sure that AutoCAD Designer does not assume your angled line to be a flat horizontal. Try to make this rough drawing look like a big plastic wiffle-ball bat. Be sure to add the fillets at each outer edge.

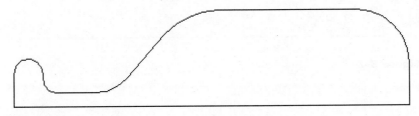

Figure 5-4

6. If your fixed point is in a different location than point P1 of Figure 5–5, move it to this location. This placement ensures that you do not run into problems constraining your sketch as you work through the following sequence of steps.

Command: **adfixpt**

Specify new fixed point for active sketch: *Pick point P1 of Figure 5–5.*

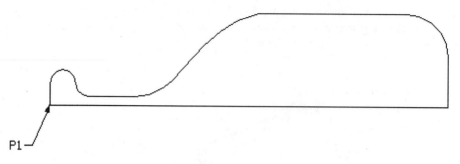

Figure 5-5

7. Make the sketch into a profile.

Command: **adprofile**

Select objects for sketch.

Select objects: *Select the entire profile.*

Select objects: ⏎

Solved under constrained sketch requiring 11 dimensions/constraints.

Note: If AutoCAD Designer turned your angled line into a flat horizontal, re-create your profile. When creating a profile, the default Designer settings assume that any line drawn at less than a four-degree angle is actually meant to be horizontal or vertical.

8. Change the current layer to Dimension.

9. Check the constraints on your profile.

Command: **adshowcon**

All/Select/Next/<eXit>: **a**

Your profile should contain the constraints shown in Figure 5–6. Add any constraints that are missing.

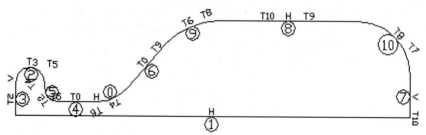

Figure 5-6

10. Dimension your profile to obtain a fully constrained sketch.

Command: **adpardim**

Select first item: *Pick arc P1 of Figure 5–7.*

Select second item or place dimension: *Pick P2.*

Undo/Hor/Ver/Align/Par/Dimension value<current>: **0.25**

Solved under constrained sketch requiring 10 dimensions/constraints.

Note: Depending on how your radii were constructed, your message may vary.

Select first item: *Pick radius P3.*

Select second item or place dimension: *Pick P4.*

Undo/Hor/Ver/Align/Par/Dimension value<current>: **2**

Solved under constrained sketch requiring 9 dimensions/constraints.

Select first item: *Pick radius P5.*

Select second item or place dimension: *Pick P6.*

Undo/Hor/Ver/Align/Par/Dimension value<current>: **2**

Solved under constrained sketch requiring 8 dimensions/constraints.

Helpful Hint: Another way of constraining radii is to use the ADADDCON command; however, we are adding individual dimensions to simplify the lesson.

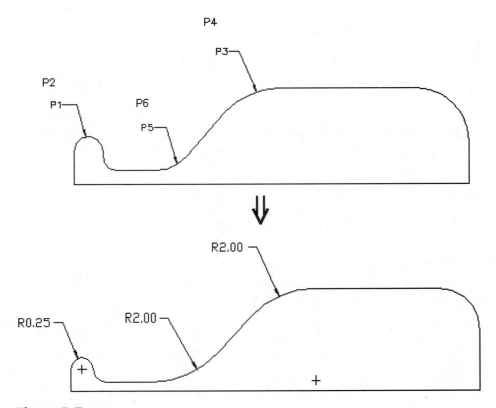

Figure 5-7

Continue dimensioning your sketch.

Select first item: *Pick radius P1 of Figure 5–8.*

Select second item or place dimension: *Pick P2.*

Undo/Hor/Ver/Align/Par/Dimension value<current>: **.25**

Solved under constrained sketch requiring 7 dimensions/constraints.

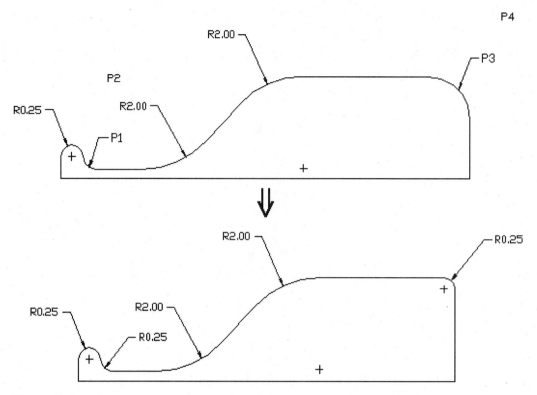

Figure 5-8

Select first item: *Pick radius P3.*

Select second item or place dimension: *Pick P4.*

Undo/Hor/Ver/Align/Par/Dimension value<current>: **.25**

Solved under constrained sketch requiring 6 dimensions/constraints.

Continue dimensioning your sketch.

Select first item: *Pick horizontal line P1 of Figure 5–9.*

Select second item or place dimension: *Pick line P2.*

Specify dimension placement: *Pick P3.*

Undo/Hor/Ver/Align/Par/Dimension value<current>: **.3**

Solved under constrained sketch requiring 5 dimensions/constraints.

Select first item: *Pick vertical line P4.*

Select second item or place dimension: *Pick P5.*

Undo/Hor/Ver/Align/Par/Dimension value<current>: **0.5**

Solved under constrained sketch requiring 4 dimensions/constraints.

Continue dimensioning your sketch.

Select first item: *Pick horizontal line P1 of Figure 5–10.*

Select second item or place dimension: *Pick P2.*

Undo/Hor/Ver/Align/Par/Dimension value<current>: **5**

Solved under constrained sketch requiring 3 dimensions/constraints.

Select first item: *Pick horizontal line P3.*

Select second item or place dimension: *Pick P4.*

Undo/Hor/Ver/Align/Par/Dimension value<current>: **3**

Solved under constrained sketch requiring 2 dimensions/constraints.

Continue dimensioning your sketch.

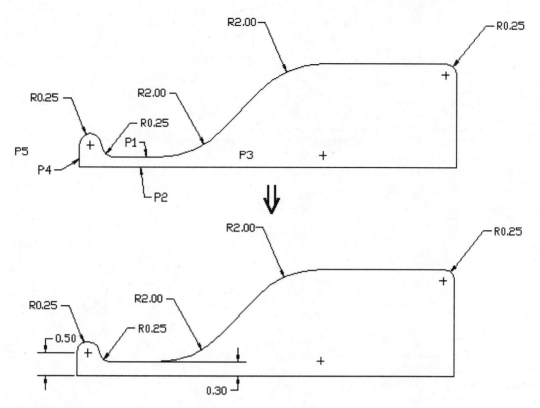

Figure 5-9

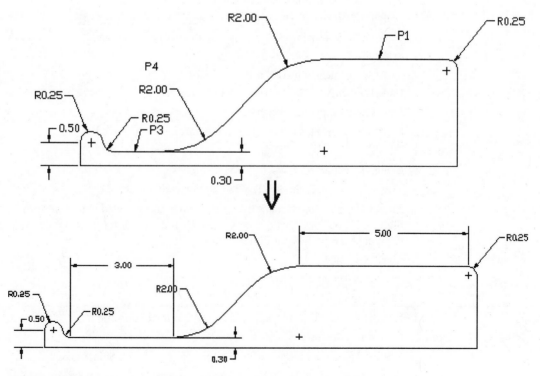

Figure 5-10

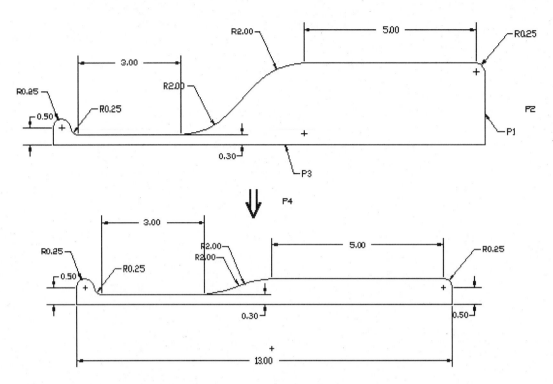

Figure 5-11

Select first item: *Pick vertical line P1 of Figure 5–11.*

Select second item or place dimension: *Pick P2.*

Undo/Hor/Ver/Align/Par/Dimension value<current>: **.5**

Solved under constrained sketch requiring 1 dimension/constraint.

Select first item: *Pick horizontal line P3.*

Select second item or place dimension: *Pick P4.*

Undo/Hor/Ver/Align/Par/Dimension value<current>: **13**

Solved fully constrained sketch.

11. Switch to an isometric view to see the part as it is revolved.

Command: **adpartview**

View option Front/Right/Left/Top/Bottom/Isometric/<Sketch>: **i**

12. This is a good point to mark the work you have completed before performing the revolution. If your bat does not look the way you want it to, you can always go back to this point to modify your dimensions.

Command: **undo**

Auto/Back/Control/End/Group/Mark/<number>: **m**

13. Change the current layer to Model.

14. Use the ADREVOLVE command to revolve the bat profile.

Command: **adrevolve**

Set the dialogue box options as shown in Figure 5–12. Select **OK**.

Select axis of revolution: *Pick the 13-unit-long centerline of the bat.*

Your revolved profile should now resemble a baseball bat, similar to that in Figure 5–13.

15. Be sure to save your work before exiting AutoCAD.

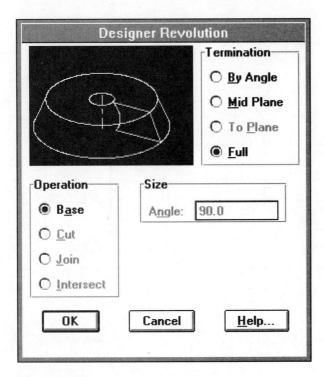

Figure 5-12

Figure 5-13

ADWORKAXIS

A work axis is a feature that is automatically constrained to pass through the centerline of a cylindrical, conical, or toroidal surface. A work axis has three main functions:

- As an axis to create a work plane through.
- As a reference line to dimension from.
- As an axis of revolution.

Command: **adworkaxis**

Select cylindrical face: *Select a cylindrical surface to create a work axis through.*

Figures 5–14 through 5–17 show the usage of work axes. In Figure 5–14 the work axes are created through the cylindrical towers.

Next, in Figure 5–15 a work plane is created through the two axes. This work plane will be our sketch plane where the next sketch is created.

Figure 5–16 illustrates a sketch being dimensioned from the work axis.

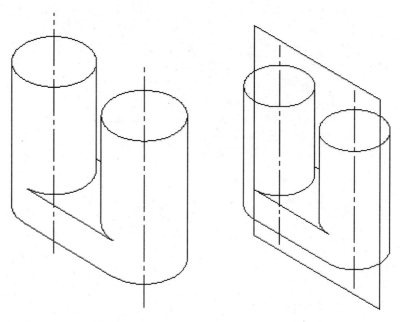

Figure 5-14   **Figure 5-15**

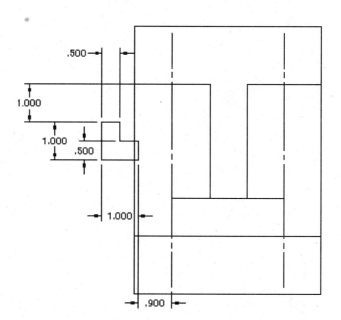

Figure 5-16

Finally, the active sketch is revolved around the work axis and joined to the model in Figure 5–17.

ADWORKAXIS TUTORIAL

This tutorial uses an extruded cylinder to place a work axis. The work axis is then used for the revolution of another feature to create a part resembling a hand weight, as shown in Figure 5–18. In Chapter 14 we make the hand weight out of different materials to show how AutoCAD Designer can actually compute the weight of a three-dimensional solid object.

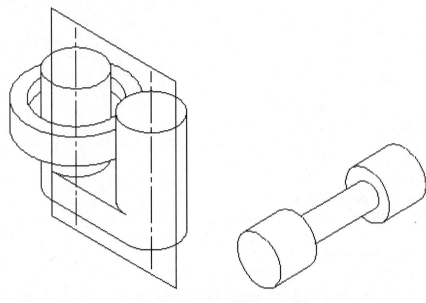

Figure 5-17   **Figure 5-18**

1. Start a new drawing in AutoCAD Designer and name it revolve2.

    Command: **new**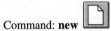

    Type **revolve2** in the New Drawing Name edit box.

    Choose **OK.**

2. Create your AutoCAD Designer layers as described in Appendix A.

3. Set Scrap as the current layer.

4. Change the isolines display for easier viewing. Optimal isoline displays vary for different models. For the hand weight, we recommend a value of 4, but you can use whatever value you are most comfortable with.

    Command: **adisolines**

    Isolines for cones, cylinders, and torii<2>: **4**

    Isolines for nurbs<0>: **0**

5. Draw a circle with an approximate diameter of 3 inches.

6. Make the circle an active profile.

    Command: **adprofile**

    Select objects for sketch.

    Select objects: *Pick the circle.*

    Select objects: ↵

    Solved under constrained sketch requiring 1 dimension/constraint.

7. Change the current layer to Dimension.

8. Dimension the profile.

    Command: **adpardim**

    Select first item: *Select the circle P1 of Figure 5–19.*

    Select second item or place dimension: *Pick near P2.*

    Undo/Dimension value <current>: **3**

    Solved fully constrained sketch.

    Select first item: ↵

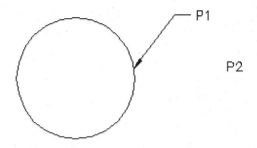

Figure 5-19

9. Change the current layer to Model.

10. Switch to an isometric view to see the part in its extruded form.

Command: **adpartview**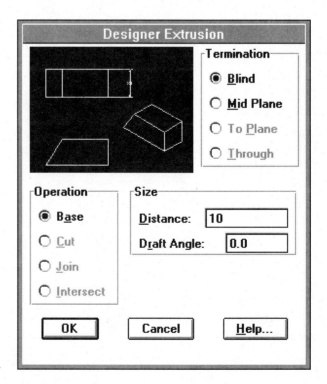

View option Front/Right/Left/Top/Bottom/Isometric/<Sketch>: **i**

11. Extrude the profile using the settings shown in Figure 5–20. This base part is the over-all size of the hand weight. The revolution performed later will cut material away to create the handle.

Figure 5-20

Your extruded profile should resemble Figure 5–21.

12. Change the current layer to Scrap.

13. You are now ready to add a work axis through the center of your cylinder. This work axis is used in creating a work plane for your sketch and is used later to revolve the profile around.

Command: **adworkaxis**

Select cylindrical face: *Select a circular portion of the cylinder.*

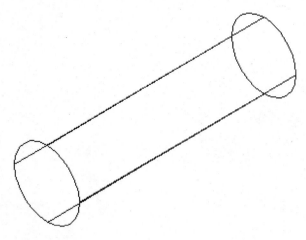

Figure 5-21

14. Use the On Edge/Axis // Planar Parallel combination to create a work plane and make it the active sketch plane. Select the options as shown in Figure 5–22. You will be using the work axis and the ZX plane to define your work plane.

    Command: **adworkpln**

    X/Y/Z/<Select work axis or straight edge>: *Select the work axis.*

    Xy/Yz/Zx/Ucs/<Select work plane or planar face>: **z**

    X/Y/Z/<Select work axis or straight edge>: **x**

    Rotate/<Accept>: ↵

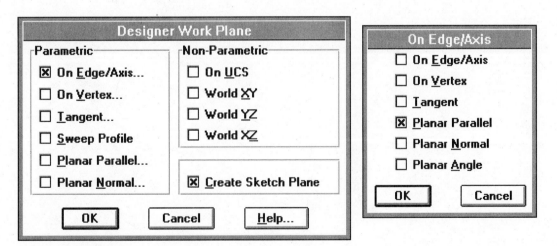

Figure 5-22

15. Keep the drawing in Isometric view and try to draw a rectangle on your model for the cut-out portion of the handle. Try to make it similar to Figure 5–23.

16. Make your rectangle the active profile.

    Command: **adprofile**

    Select objects for sketch.

    Select objects: *Select the rectangle.*

    Select objects: ↵

    Solved under constrained sketch requiring 4 dimensions/constraints.

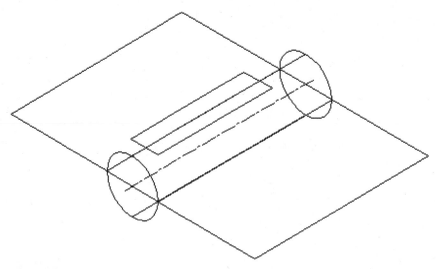

Figure 5-23

17. Switch the current layer to Dimension.

18. Check to see that your profile contains the constraints shown in Figure 5–24. Add any missing constraints.

    Command: **adshowcon**

    All/Select/Next/<eXit>: **a**

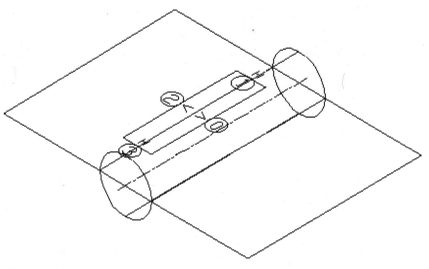

Figure 5-24

19. Switch the dimension display to Equations to show both the dimension variable and actual dimension value.

    Command: **addimdsp**

    Parameters/Equations/<Numeric>: **e**

20. Constrain the profile dimensionally. It may be necessary to use your Zoom command to help view specific portions of the profile.

    Command: **adpardim**

    Select first item: *Pick on line P1 of Figure 5–25.*

    Select second item or place dimension: *Pick on cylinder P2.*

Specify dimension placement: *Pick near point P3.*

Undo/Hor/Ver/Align/Par/Dimension value <current>: **2.5**

Solved under constrained sketch requiring 3 dimensions/constraints.

Select first item: *Pick opposite end of rectangle P4.*

Select second item or place dimension: *Pick cylinder P5.*

Specify dimension placement: *Pick near P6.*

Undo/Hor/Ver/Align/Par/Dimension value <current>: **d3**

Solved under constrained sketch requiring 2 dimensions/constraints.

We have just set both ends of the hand weight equal in length. If the 2.5 dimension needs to be changed in the future, both ends will be kept equal automatically.

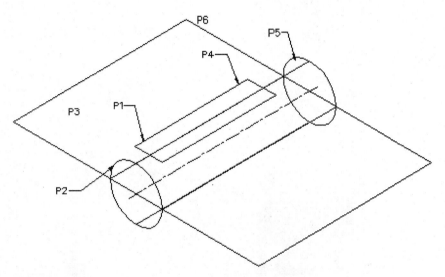

Figure 5-25

Continue dimensioning your sketch.

Select first item: *Pick on line P1 of Figure 5–26.*

Select second item or place dimension: *Pick on the cylinder P2.*

Specify dimension placement: *Pick near P3.*

Undo/Hor/Ver/Align/Par/Dimension value <current>: **.75**

Solved under constrained sketch requiring 1 dimension/constraint.

Select first item: *Pick line P1.*

Select second item or place dimension: *Pick near P4.*

Undo/Hor/Ver/Align/Par/Dimension value <current>: **1.5**

Solved fully constrained sketch.

Select first item: ↵

Notice that the profile's width continues beyond the outside of the cylinder, which is possible because we are cutting away material from the part. With no material beyond the circumference of the circle, we are not cutting away anything extra.

21. Once again, switch the current layer to Model.

22. Revolve the profile around the work axis; use the settings shown in Figure 5–27.

    Command: **adrevolve**

    Select axis of revolution: *Select the work axis.*

    Your hand weight should now look similar to the drawing in Figure 5–28.

23. Save your work for future reference.

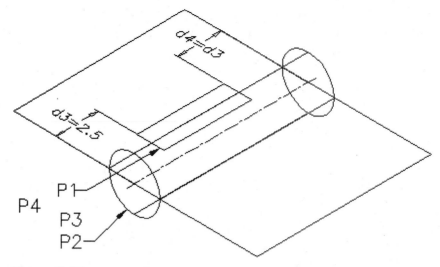

Figure 5-26

Figure 5-27

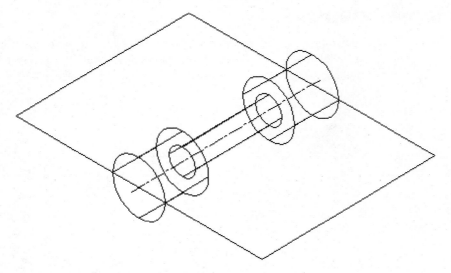

Figure 5-28

ADAXISDSP

ADAXISDSP toggles the display of the work axes. If ADAXISDSP is turned on, the axes will be displayed. If you wish to create a work plane through a work axis or edit a dimension that is from a work axis, your axis display must be on.

> Command: **adaxisdsp**
>
> Off/<On>: *Select an option.*

ADAXISDSP TUTORIAL

Try turning off the work axis created in the previous tutorial.

1. Open the previously created drawing.

   Command: **open**

   Open revolve2.dwg by selecting the correct drive and directory and then selecting the file.

   Choose **OK.**

2. Turn off the work axis.

   Command: **adaxisdsp**

   ON/OFF: **off**

   Do not resave the drawing with the work axis turned off.

REVIEW QUESTIONS

5.1   Compare and contrast the ADREVOLVE feature command with the ADEX-TRUDE feature command. What are the similarities? What are the differences?

5.2   List the valid axes of rotation for a revolution.

5.3   List the various operations that the ADREVOLVE feature command can perform. Briefly explain each operation.

5.4   How does the termination of a revolution vary from that of an extrusion? For the revolution, list the four termination types and briefly explain each one.

5.5   Define a work axis.

5.6   In what ways can a work axis be used to assist in creating a feature?

CHAPTER EXERCISES

5.1–5.12   From the two-dimensional profiles provided, create the revolved feature using the y-axis as the axis of revolution. Check to see that your revolved part matches one of the isometric drawings in Figure Exer 5–1 to Figure Exer 5–12.

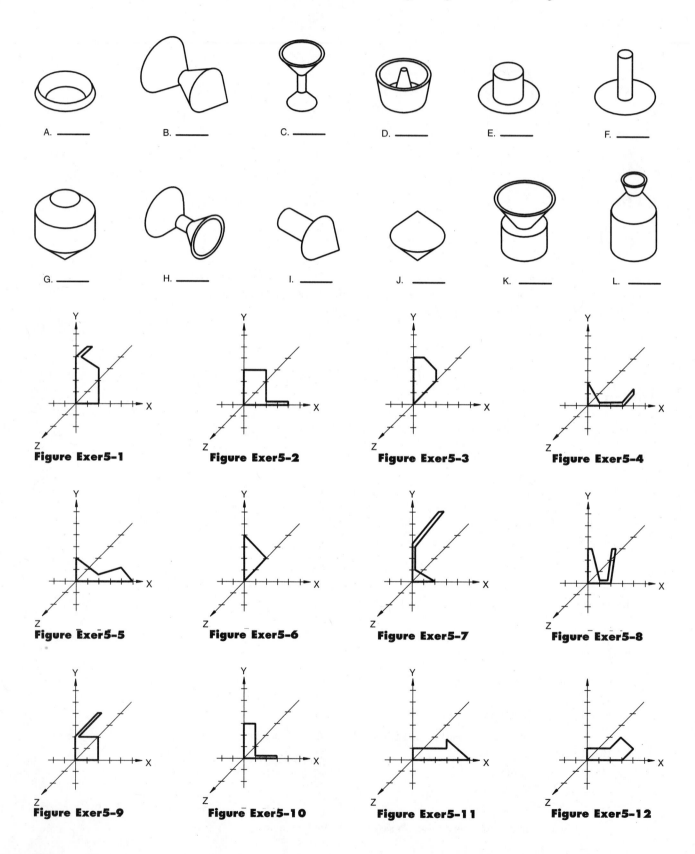

A. ____   B. ____   C. ____   D. ____   E. ____   F. ____

G. ____   H. ____   I. ____   J. ____   K. ____   L. ____

Figure Exer5-1   Figure Exer5-2   Figure Exer5-3   Figure Exer5-4

Figure Exer5-5   Figure Exer5-6   Figure Exer5-7   Figure Exer5-8

Figure Exer5-9   Figure Exer5-10   Figure Exer5-11   Figure Exer5-12

5.13   From the fully dimensioned isometric drawing, create the wheel in Figure Exer 5–13. Use revolve techniques.

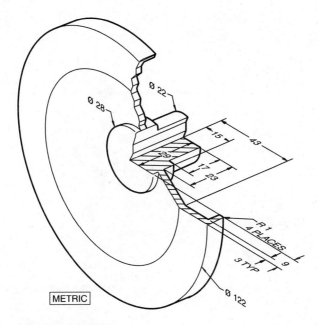

Figure Exer5-13

5.14   From the fully dimensioned isometric drawing, create the retainer in Figure Exer 5–14. Use revolve techniques and a single extrusion.

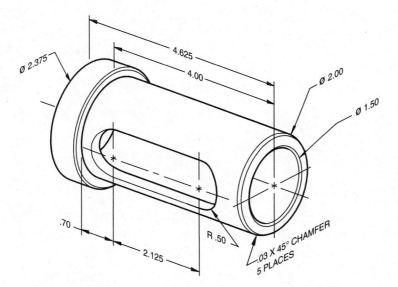

Figure Exer5-14

5.15   From the fully dimensioned isometric drawing, create the half pin in Figure Exer 5–15. Use revolve techniques.

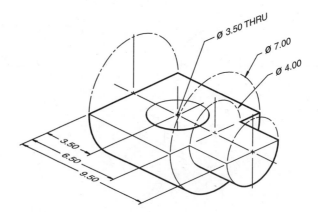

Figure Exer5-15

5.16   From the fully dimensioned isometric drawing, create the timing knob in Figure Exer 5–16. Use revolve techniques.

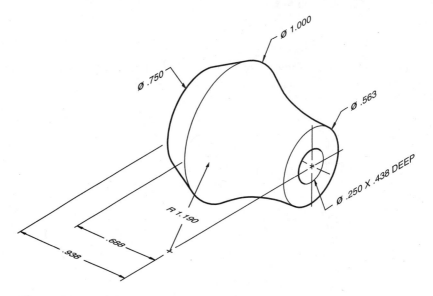

Figure Exer5-16

5.17   From the fully dimensioned isometric drawing, create the profile of the transition in Figure Exer5–17 and revolve it around its center axis.

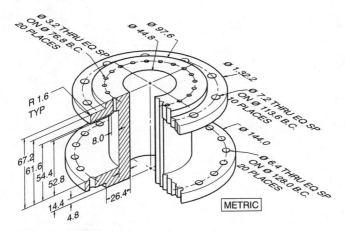

Figure Exer5-17

5.18   From the fully dimensioned isometric drawing, create the oil transfer in Figure Exer5–18. Use revolve techniques.

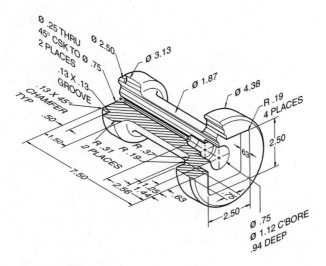

Figure Exer5-18

SWEEPS

A sweep feature is created by taking a two-dimensional profile and sweeping it along a user-defined path. The **ADSWEEP** command allows you to combine what may be several segments of a part by using a mix of the ADEXTRUDE and ADREVOLVE commands. Think of a chain link. One link requires two extrusions and two revolutions constrained to each other to make a single solid link. The sweep feature, however, can create the one-link part with only a single cross-sectional profile and a defined path for the profile to sweep along. Figure 6–1 shows how this combination of a profile and path can produce the final sweep feature.

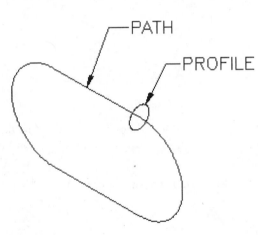
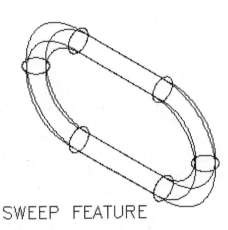

Figure 6–1

ADPATH

The **ADPATH** command is used in conjunction with the ADPROFILE command to create a sweep feature. Paths are very similar to profiles except that in paths the two-dimensional geometry may be open, as shown in Figure 6–2. The methods of dimensioning and constraining are the same for paths and profiles.

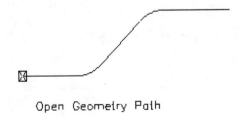
Open Geometry Path

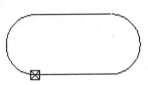
Closed Geometry Path

Figure 6–2

Command: **adpath**

Select objects for sketch: *Select the two-dimensional sketch.*

Specify start point of path: *Pick near one of the open ends of your path. Note: This line will not appear if your path has closed geometry.*

Figure 6–3 shows how the path is used with the cross-sectional profile sweeping along it to create a three-dimensional solid model. The sequence of commands to create a sweep feature follows:

1. Use ADPATH to create a path for the profile to follow along.
2. Use ADPROFILE to create a cross-sectional profile to be swept along the path.
3. Use ADSWEEP to sweep the selected profile along the path.

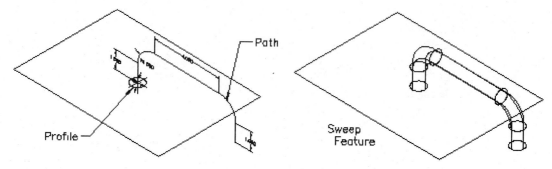

Figure 6-3

ADPATH TUTORIAL

This lesson gets you started on the first portion (the path) of a two-part tutorial that shows you how to use a normal sweep through AutoCAD Designer to make a chain link. Your completed model will look like Figure 6–4.

1. Begin a new drawing in AutoCAD Designer and name it sweep1.

Command: **new**

Type **sweep1** in the New Drawing Name edit box.

Choose **OK.**

2. Create your AutoCAD Designer layers as described in Appendix A.

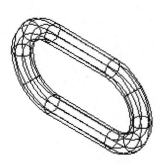

Figure 6-4

3. Change your isolines display for easier viewing. Remember, you won't benefit from this change until the model is created in the following tutorial.

Command: **adisolines**

Isolines for cones, cylinders, and torii <2>: **8**

Isolines for nurbs <0>: ⏎

4. Set Scrap as the current layer

5. Sketch the oval shown in Figure 6–5. Remember, it doesn't have to be exact. AutoCAD Designer will take care of that for you.

Figure 6-5

6. Create a path from the oval.

   Command: **adpath**

   Select objects for sketch.

   Select objects: *Select the oval you just created.*

   Select objects: ↵

   Solved under constrained sketch requiring 2 dimensions/constraints.

   Note: Your message may vary slightly.

7. Verify your constraints.

   Command: **adshowcon**

   All/Select/Next/<eXit>: **a**

   If your path does not contain all the constraints shown in Figure 6–6, add the ones you are missing.

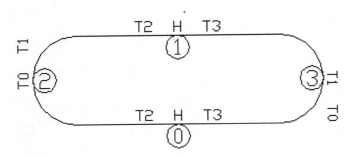

Figure 6-6

8. Set Dimension as the current layer.

9. Dimensionally constrain your path just like you would constrain a profile.

   Command: **adpardim**

   Select first item: *Pick P1 of Figure 6–7.*

   Select second item or place dimension: *Pick P2.*

   Undo/Dimension value <current>: **.5**

   Solved under constrained sketch requiring 1 dimension/constraint.

   Select first item: *Pick P3.*

   Select second item or place dimension: *Pick P4.*

   Undo/Dimension value <current>: **1.00**

   Solved fully constrained sketch.

   Select first item: ↵

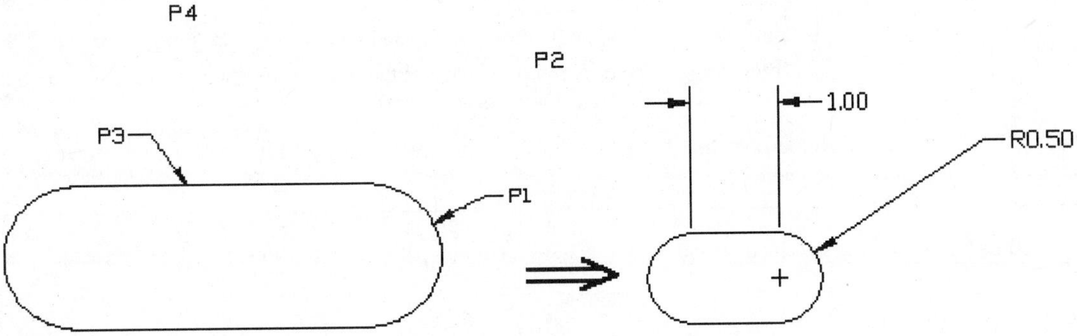

Figure 6-7

10. Save your work to use in the next half of this tutorial.

ADSWEEP

Now that you know how to create both a profile and a path, you are ready to use the ADSWEEP feature command. With the ADREVOLVE feature command, the profile was revolved around an axis. Here, using the ADSWEEP feature command, the profile sweeps along a path to produce a solid geometric feature. Figure 6–8 shows the two different types of sweep features that you can create.

Command: **adsweep**

Select sweep path: *Pick on the sketch path.*

Select sweep cross section profile: *Pick on the sketch profile.*

Parallel/<Normal>: *Select an option depending on how you want the profile configured along the path.*

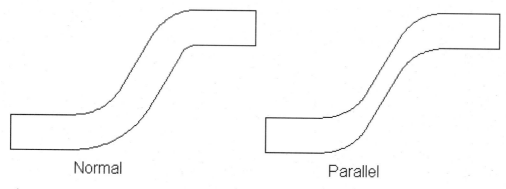

Normal   Parallel

Figure 6–8

Parallel   This option keeps the profile parallel to the sketch plane as it is swept along the path.

Normal   This option keeps the profile normal to the sweep path as it is swept along the path. Most of the parts you create will use this configuration, as most solids do not have a parallel geometry. If your path contains only lines or **polylines** and is perpendicular to the profile, you may specify a draft angle.

Draft Angle (positive tapers out) <0>: *Enter a draft angle in degrees.*

Leaving the default value of 0 creates the part without draft. Finally, if you are expanding on an existing active part, AutoCAD Designer will prompt you with an operation similar to those found in the dialogue boxes described earlier. The ADSWEEP command allows you to add or remove material from the active part.

Cut/Join/<Intersect>: *Choose an operation.*

Cut   Just like previous features, the Cut operation removes material from the active part.

Join   This option allows you to add material to an existing active part.

Intersect   Intersect removes material that lies outside the volume of the current sweep feature from the existing part.

Remember that the ADSWEEP command requires both a path and a profile.

Helpful Hint: Do not use the sweep command when you have a circular path; use the revolve command instead.

ADSWEEP TUTORIAL

We will now continue making our chain link where we left off with the ADPATH tutorial. This tutorial covers constraining the profile to the path and then using the ADSWEEP command.

1. Open the drawing created in the last tutorial.

    Command: **open**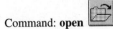

    Open sweep1.dwg by selecting the drive and directory of the file and then selecting the file.

    Choose **OK.**

2. Change to an isometric view.

    Command: **adpartview**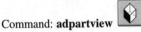

    View option Front/Right/Left/Top/Bottom/Isometric/<Sketch>: **i** ↵

3. Add a workplane to the path and make it the active sketch plane to create the sweep profile.

    Command: **adworkpln**

    Select sweep profile and sketch plane from the dialogue box.

    Choose **OK.**

    Select an item in the path: *Select the oval that you just created.*

    Rotate the UCS icon until the y-axis is pointing upward and then accept. See Figure 6–9.

    Note: If your plane does not appear, turn on your plane display.

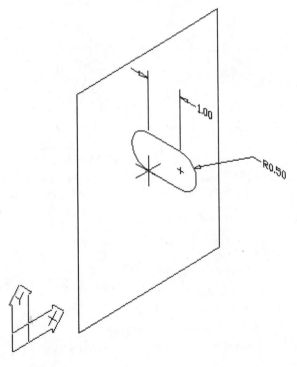

Figure 6-9

4. Return to a sketch view to create your profile.

    Command: **adpartview**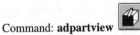

    View option Front/Right/Left/Top/Bottom/Isometric/<Sketch>: *Enter to accept the default sketch.*

5. Set Scrap layer as current.

6. Draw a circle on the sketch plane as shown in Figure 6–10.

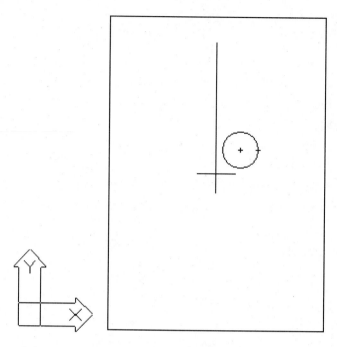

Figure 6-10

7. Let AutoCAD Designer know that you want the circle as your profile.

Command: **adprofile**

Select objects for sketch.

Select objects: *Select the circle.*

Select objects: ↵

Solved under constrained sketch requiring 1 dimension/constraint.

Note: Although AutoCAD Designer told you it needs only one dimension/constraint, you also must dimension it to your path. Watch what happens to your dimension/constraint count.

8. Constrain your profile to your path.

Command: **adpardim**

Select first item: *Pick P1 of Figure 6–11.*

Select second item or place dimension: *Pick P2.*

Specify dimension placement: *Pick P3.*

Undo/Hor/Ver/Align/Par/Dimension value <current>: **0**

Solved under constrained sketch requiring 2 dimensions/constraints.

Select first item: *Pick P1.*

Select second item or place dimension: *Pick circle P2.*

Undo/Hor/Ver/Align/Par/Dimension value <current>: **0**

Solved under constrained sketch requiring 1 dimension/constraint.

Select first item: *Pick circle P2.*

Select second item or place dimension: *Pick P4.*

Undo/Dimension value <current>: **.25**

Solved fully constrained sketch.

Select first item. ↵

9. Return to an isometric view.

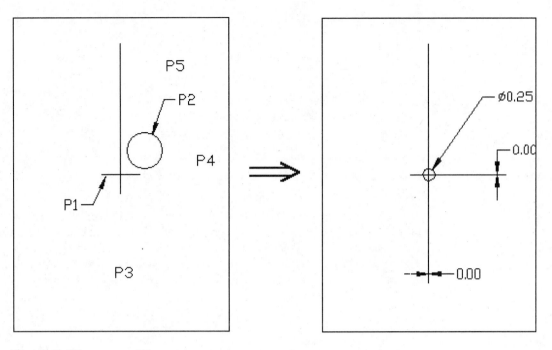

Figure 6-11

Command: **adpartview**

View option Front/Right/Left/Top/Bottom/Isometric/<Sketch>: **i**

10. Turn off your work plane because you don't need it anymore.
    Command: **adplndsp**
    OFf/<ON>: **off**

11. Zoom in on your path and profile. They should now resemble Figure 6–12.

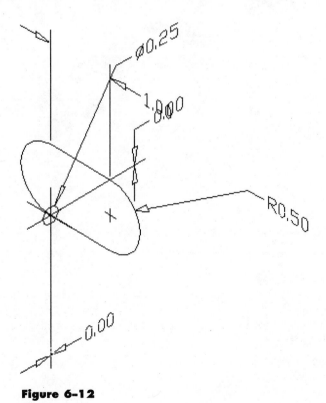

Figure 6-12

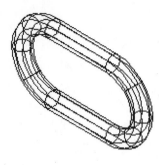

Figure 6-13

12. Switch the current layer to Model.

13. Create your sweep feature.

Command: **adsweep**

Select sweep path: *Select the oval.*

Oblique, non-uniformly scaled entities were ignored.

Select sweep cross section profile: *Select the circle.*

Parallel/<Normal>: *Press return to accept the default Normal.*

Your completed sweep should look like Figure 6–13.

14. Before exiting AutoCAD be sure to save your work.

From the creation of one chain link, you can then use AutoCAD's copy and rotate commands to create a longer chain as shown in Figure 6–14. Keep in mind, however, that these copied links are no longer parametric and cannot be changed like standard AutoCAD Designer features. These copied features lose all of the original parts properties and cannot be meshed or rendered. In Chapter 15 we show you how to lengthen the chain while maintaining AutoCAD Designer parametric properties.

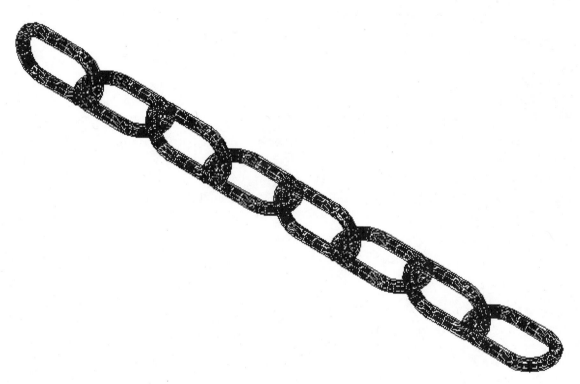

Figure 6-14

REVIEW QUESTIONS

6.1   What are the two main elements needed to create a sweep feature?

6.2   Compare and contrast a path and a profile. What are the similarities and what are the differences?

6.3   To create a sweep feature, which needs to be created first: the path or the profile? Explain why.

6.4   What are the two types of sweep features? How are they different?

6.5   In addition to the chain link, describe two parts that could not be created with a single extrusion or revolution but could be constructed with the sweep feature.

CHAPTER EXERCISES

6.1   From the fully dimensioned isometric drawing, use normal sweep techniques to create the handle in Figure Exer6–1.

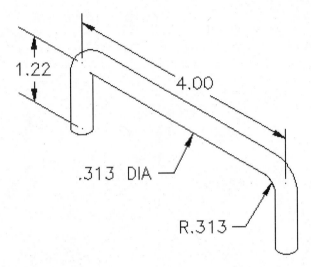

Figure Exer6-1

6.2   From the fully defined path and profile, use normal sweep techniques to create the protector in Figure Exer6–2.

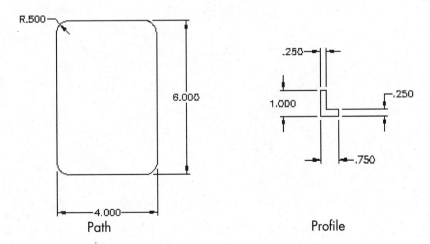

Figure Exer6-2

6.3   From the fully defined path and profile, use normal sweep techniques to create the slide rod in Figure Exer6–3.

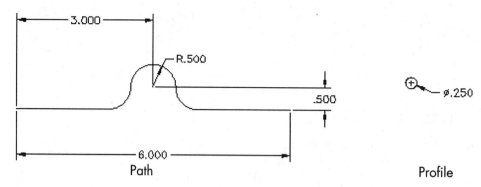

Figure Exer6-3

6.4   From the fully defined path and profile of Exercise 6.3, use parallel sweep techniques to create the slide rod in Figure Exer6–3.

chapter

7

HOLES AND POINTS

This chapter looks at a simplified method of adding holes to existing active parts. This group of commands allows you to use various methods of placement, including **work points,** to add just about any type of hole, such as drilled, counterbored, and countersunk, to existing active parts.

ADHOLE

ADHOLE creates drilled holes in the active part. One of this feature's options is the ability to make specified counterbores and countersinks. Holes can also be created with ADEXTRUDE or even ADREVOLVE; however, the ADHOLE command is generally much more efficient. Figure 7–1 shows a block with two counterbored holes that were added with the ADHOLE feature command.

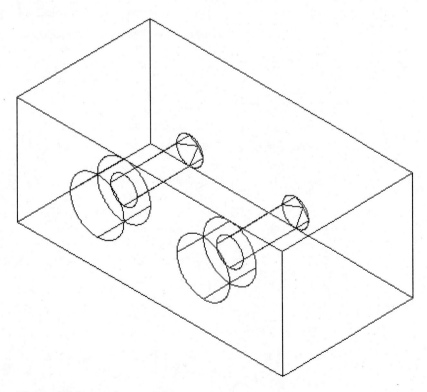

Figure 7-1

Command: **adhole**

After you type the ADHOLE command, the Designer Hole dialogue box shown in Figure 7–2 appears.

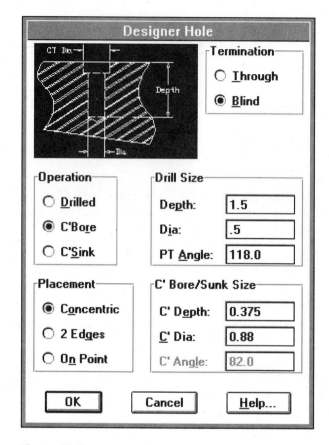

Figure 7-2

Operation   Specifies the type of hole.

  Drilled   Creates a specified-diameter hole in the active part.

  C'Bore   Creates a specified-diameter hole in the part with a dimensionally specified counterbore added.

  C'Sink   Creates a specified-diameter hole in the part with a dimensionally specified countersink added.

Placement   Specifies the hole's location with one of three simple placement options. Unlike the previous features, the ADHOLE command does not use a dimensionally constrained sketch. Instead, holes are fully defined in the dialogue box.

  Concentric   Locates the hole by making it concentric with a selected curved face. The hole will be drilled along the axis of the selected curve, perpendicular to the planar face or work plane.

    X/Y/Z/Ucs/Select work plane or planar face: *Select the plane.*

    Select concentric edge: *Pick the curved edge that the hole is to be concentric with.*

  2 Edges   Locates the hole a specified distance from two edges of a common face. If the hole is to be placed on the corner of a block, you can specify the hole to be 2 inches off one edge and 1.75 inches off the other.

    Select first edge: *Pick the first edge that the hole is to be offset from.*

    Select second edge: *Pick the second edge that the hole is to be offset from.*

Select hole location: *Pick inside the two selected edges.*

Distance from first edge <current>: *Type in the specified distance from the first edge or hit return to accept the default value.*

Distance from second edge <current>: *Type in the specified distance from the second edge or hit return to accept the default value.*

On Point   Locates the hole on a specified work point (described later in this chapter) and directs it along an axis perpendicular to the sketch plane of the work point. You must create and define the position of the work point prior to using the ADHOLE command.

Select work point: *Pick the previously defined work point.*

Direction Flip/<Accept> *Select option according to the direction in which you want the hole to be drilled.*

Termination   Determines the depth of the hole. Both of these termination methods are identical to the methods used with the ADEXTRUDE command.

Through   Starting from the selected planar surface, this option continues the hole through the solid part.

Blind   This method of termination allows you to set a numeric depth for the hole.

Drill Size   Specifies various measurements for the hole.

Depth   Type the overall depth of the hole.

Dia   Type the drill bit size or the diameter of the hole.

PT Angle   Drill bits have angled tips. Type in the angle for the point at the bottom of the hole. This option is not valid for through holes.

C' Bore/Sunk Size   Specifies the size of the counterbore or countersink if one of these options is chosen.

C' Depth   Type in the depth of the counterbore for the counterbore operation.

C' Dia   Type in the outer diameter of either the counterbore or countersink.

C' Angle   Type in the angle of the countersink for the countersink operation.

ADHOLE Tutorial

This lesson demonstrates the use of the ADHOLE command by beginning with a simple block and adding holes with the various options. The model you create from this tutorial should resemble the block shown in Figure 7–3.

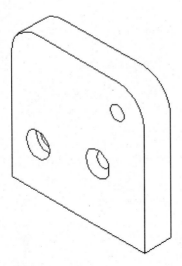

Figure 7-3

1. Start a new drawing in AutoCAD Designer and name it hole1.

   Command: **new**

   Type **hole1** in the New Drawing Name edit box.

   Choose **OK.**

2. Create your AutoCAD Designer layers as described in Appendix A.

3. Change your isolines display for easier viewing.

   Command: **adisolines**

   Isolines for cones, cylinders, and torii <2>: **4**

   Isolines for nurbs <0>: ↵

4. Set Scrap as the current layer.

5. Sketch a block similar to that shown in Figure 7–4.

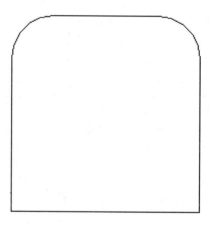

Figure 7-4

6. Make the sketch into a profile.

   Command: **adprofile**

   Select objects for sketch.

   Select objects: *Select the entire block.*

   Select objects: ↵

   Solved under constrained sketch requiring 4 dimensions/constraints.

   Note: Your message may vary slightly.

7. Check the constraints on your profile.

   Command: **adshowcon**

   All/Select/Next/<eXit>: **a**

   Your profile should contain the constraints shown in Figure 7–5. Add any constraints that are missing.

8. Change the current layer to Dimension.

9. Dimension your profile.

   Command: **adpardim**

   Select first item: *Pick vertical line P1 of Figure 7–6.*

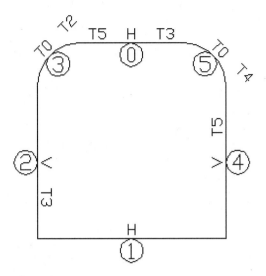

Figure 7-5

Select second item or place dimension: *Pick horizontal line P2.*

Specify dimension placement: *Pick P3.*

Undo/Hor/Ver/Align/Par/Dimension value<current>: **5**

Solved under constrained sketch requiring 3 dimensions/constraints.

Select first item: *Pick horizontal line P4.*

Select second item or place dimension: *Pick P5.*

Undo/Hor/Ver/Align/Par/Dimension value<current>: **5**

Solved under constrained sketch requiring 2 dimensions/constraints.

Select first item: *Pick radius P6.*

Select second item or place dimension: *Pick P7.*

Undo/Dimension value<current>: **1**

Solved under constrained sketch requiring 1 dimension/constraint.

Note: If your sketch is fully constrained, skip to step 10.

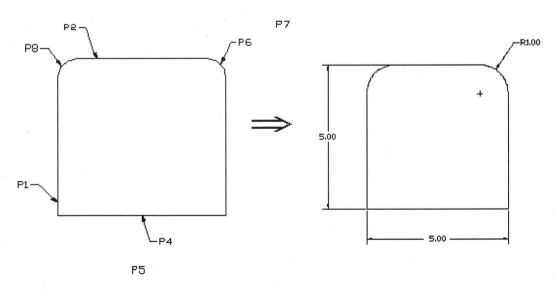

Figure 7-6

Select first item: ↵

Command: **adaddcon**

Hor/Ver/PErp/PAr/Tan/CL/CN/Proj/Join/XValue/Yvalue/Radius/<eXit>: **r**

Select first arc or circle: *Pick radius P6.*

Select second arc or circle: *Pick radius P8.*

Solved fully constrained sketch.

Hor/Ver/PErp/PAr/Tan/CL/CN/Proj/Join/XValue/Yvalue/Radius/<eXit>: ↵

10. Switch to Isometric view to view the part as it is extruded.

Command: **adpartview**

View option Front/Right/Left/Top/Bottom/Isometric/<Sketch>: **i**

11. Set the current layer to Model.

12. Extrude the profile.

Command: **adextrude**

Set the Designer Extrusion dialogue box options as shown in Figure 7–7 then select **OK**.

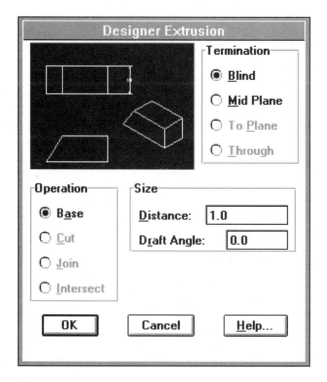

Figure 7-7

13. You are now ready to begin inserting some holes into your block. Use the AutoCAD Designer pull-down menus or type in the ADHOLE command to display the Designer Hole dialogue box.

Command: **adhole**

Notice the various options provided in the Designer Hole dialogue box. Click on each operation to get a visual picture of the types of holes you can create. The various placement options are the main focus of this exercise. Start with the concentric placement option and set the remainder of your settings to match those in Figure 7–8.

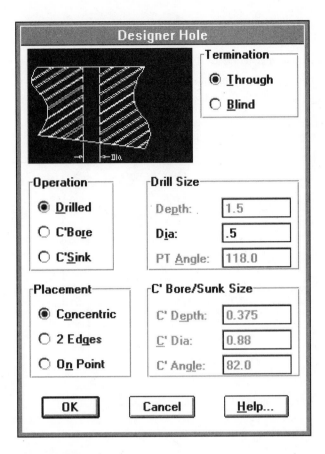

Figure 7-8

Select work plane or planar face: *Pick P1 of Figure 7–9.*

Select concentric edge: *Pick P1 again.*

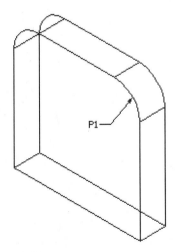

Figure 7-9

14. Your block should look similar to that of Figure 7–10. Now try the operation with the placement option set to 2 Edges and the hole type set to Counterbore. Leave the other options set to their defaults.

Command: **adhole**

Select first edge: *Pick P1 of Figure 7–10.*

Select second edge: *Pick P2.*

Select hole location: *Pick anywhere inside the block.*

Distance from first edge <current>: **1**

Distance from second edge <current>: **1.5**

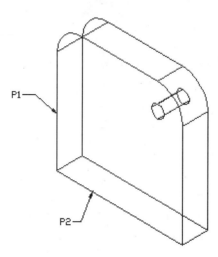

Figure 7-10

At this point, your block should resemble Figure 7–11.

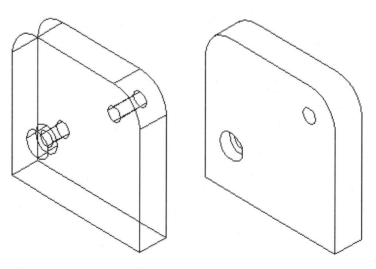

Figure 7-11

15. Save your work. You will continue adding holes to the block using other placement techniques in the ADWORKPT tutorial.

ADWORKPT

ADWORKPT creates work points for the construction of hole features. The only function of work points is to locate the center of a hole for the ADHOLE feature command. Work points must be placed on a sketch plane just like any other feature, and they must be fully constrained with X and Y dimensions in order to be edited parametrically.

Command: **adworkpt**

Location on sketch plane: *Select a location on the current sketch plane on which to place a work point.*

Work points are extremely useful when hole features cannot be created using the concentric or two-edges options. A practical application is to use work points along with geometry to place holes around a bolt circle. Geometric equations can be used in the work-point dimensioning process to fully define the hole location. Figure 7–12 shows a work point being dimensioned according to a bolt circle. In this example the desired bolt circle radius is 1.00, and it is intended that eight holes be equally spaced around the bolt circle.

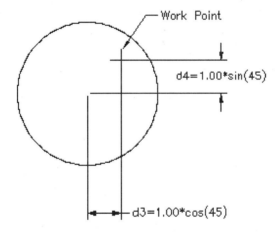

Figure 7-12

The other seven holes can be created as follows:

1. Continue to create the work points as described previously until all of them have been fully constrained. Figure 7–13 shows the eight work points located around the bolt circle. Dimensions have been removed to avoid clutter.

2. Repeat the ADHOLE command eight times to create the holes. Figure 7–14 shows the final bolt circle.

Until the ADHOLE command is used, use the ADMODDIM command to edit any of the work point's dimensions. After ADHOLE is used, work points become like other features in that you use the ADEDITFEAT command to edit the dimensions.

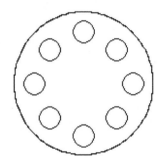

Figure 7-13

ADWORKPT Tutorial

This tutorial continues with the block created in the previous tutorial and introduces the work-point placement technique.

1. Open the drawing you created in the last tutorial.

Command: **open**

Open hole1.dwg by selecting the drive and directory of the file and then selecting the file.
Choose **OK.**

2. The distance from an edge or being concentric with a curve is not always the method you will need to place a hole. With the ON POINT placement option, the hole can be located anywhere on the sketch plane, while the other two placement options require the hole to be either concentric with a curved surface or a set distance from two edges of your model. With the ON POINT placement option, any of the features of the current part can be used for reference in dimensioning the point's placement. Before using the ADHOLE command, make the front face of the block the current sketch plane and set the current layer to Dimension.

Figure 7-14

Command: **adskpln**

Xy/Yz/Zx/Ucs/<Select work plane or planar face>: *Pick P1 of Figure 7–15.*

Select another edge: *Pick P2.*

X/Y/Z/<Select work axis or straight edge>: **x**

Rotate/<Accept>: ↵

3. Set Dimension as the current layer.

4. Add a work point from which your third hole will be created.

Command: **adworkpt**

Location on sketch plane: *Pick P3.*

Work point requires 2 dimensions and/or constraints.

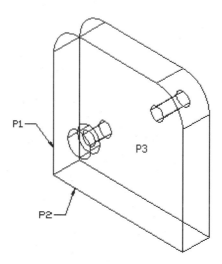

Figure 7-15

5. Constrain your work point just as you would a profile.

Command: **adpardim**

Select first item: *Pick P1 of Figure 7–16.*

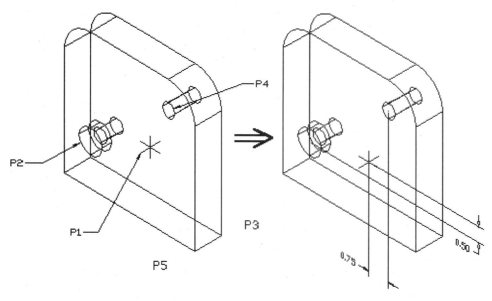

Figure 7-16

Select second item or place dimension: *Pick P2.*

Specify dimension placement: *Pick P3.*

Undo/Hor/Ver/Align/Par/Dimension value<current>: **.5**

Solved under constrained sketch requiring 1 dimension/constraint.

Select first item: *Pick P1.*

Select second item or place dimension: *Pick P4.*

Specify dimension placement: *Pick P5.*

Undo/Hor/Ver/Align/Par/Dimension value<current>: **.75**

Solved fully constrained sketch.

Select first item: ↵

6. Add your last hole. The placement option should be set to ON POINT and the operation should be set to C'SINK. Leave the other settings at their defaults.

    Command: **adhole**

    Select work point: *Pick the work point you just created.*

7. Your block should now resemble that of Figure 7–17. Now that you have an understanding of the placement options, try changing some of the various settings in the dialogue box and creating additional holes until you feel comfortable with the options.

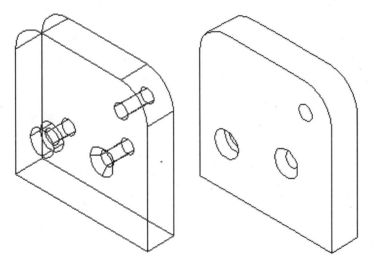

Figure 7-17

8. Save your drawing before you exit AutoCAD.

ADPTDSP

ADPTDSP toggles the display of work points. If ADPTDSP is turned on, the points are displayed. In order to edit an existing work point or construct a hole on a work point, ADPTDSP needs to be set to ON.

    Command: **adptdsp**

    Off/<On>: *Select an option.*

The ADPTDSP command is similar to the ADAXISDSP and ADPLNDSP commands, yet the ADPTDSP command is used much less frequently. This is because the work point is only used once to locate a hole. After the hole is created, the work point automatically disappears. A tutorial is not given for this command, but if you wish to try using the command open the hole1 drawing, add a point, and use the ADPTDSP command to turn the point off and on.

REVIEW QUESTIONS

7.1   What types of holes can you make with the ADHOLE feature command?

7.2   Describe the three different methods of locating a hole on the active part.

7.3   If your model was a basic square shape with no round surfaces, which of the three methods would probably be easiest for locating a hole on the model?

7.4   Which method of locating a hole in a model is the least restricted when it comes to defining the hole's location? Explain why.

7.5   What is the point angle of a drilled hole?

7.6   With AutoCAD Designer features such as ADEXTRUDE and ADREVOLVE, only one profile can be defined before it is either extruded or revolved. How many work points can be added to a model before the ADHOLE feature command is used?

7.7   Do work points need to be placed on the sketch planes?

CHAPTER EXERCISES

7.1   Add a drilled hole to the center of each end of the handle created in Exercise 6.1. Dia = 0.125, Depth = 0.5.

7.2   Add six counterbored holes in the locations shown in Figure Exer7–2 to the protector created in Exercise 6.2. Dia = 0.125, C'Depth = 0.1, C'Dia = .25.

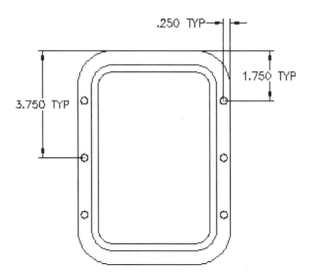

Figure Exer7-2

7.3   Add eight equally spaced 10-millimeter-diameter through holes to the wheel created in Exercise 5.13. Place the center of the holes 9 millimeters from the outer edge.

7.4   Add the holes shown in Exercise 5.17 to the base of the transition created in that exercise.

chapter
8

CHAMFER AND FILLET

The final two AutoCAD Designer features, chamfer and fillet, can be added only to existing active parts. These two features are useful design tools that can be used to either eliminate a stress concentration or simply remove a sharp edge. AutoCAD Designer makes these features easy to add; you simply define a chamfer or fillet size in a dialogue box and pick an edge for the feature to be applied to.

ADCHAMFER

ADCHAMFER places a chamfer along a selected edge or edges of the active part as shown in Figure 8–1. This figure shows a chamfer being applied to four separate edges of a block. Similar to the **ADFILLET** command described later in the chapter, **ADCHAMFER** allows a single selected entity to include more than one edge if the endpoints of joining edges are tangent.

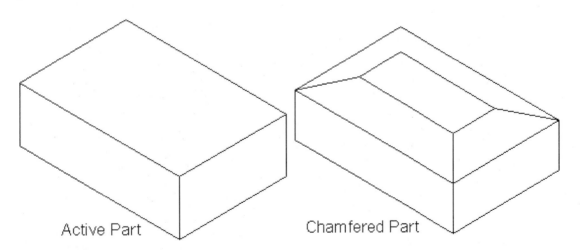

Active Part   Chamfered Part

Figure 8-1

Command: **adchamfer**

The Designer Chamfer dialogue box shown in Figure 8–2 appears when you enter this command.

Operation   Determines how the chamfer will be defined.

   Equal Distance   This method creates a standard 45-degree chamfer with the size of the chamfer specified by one distance.

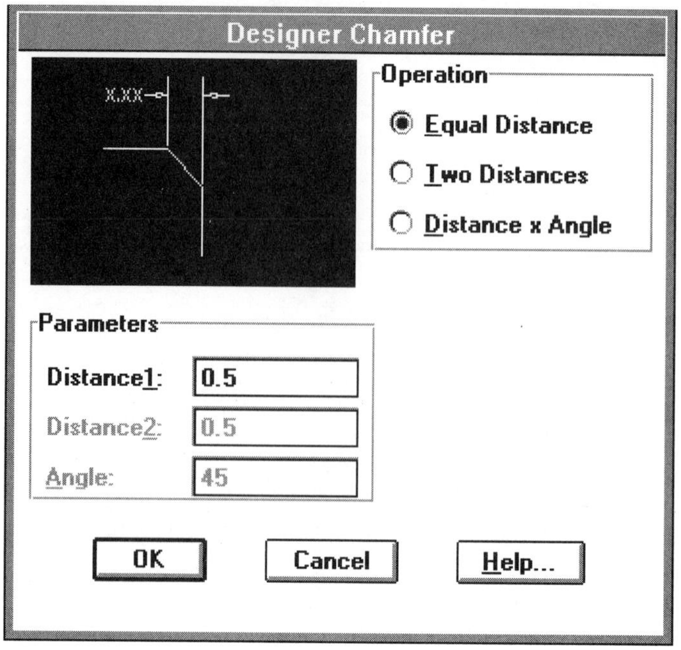

Figure 8-2

Select edge: *Select the edge you want to chamfer.*

Select edge: *Select additional edges or press ↵ to continue.*

Two Distances   Creates a chamfer specified by two distances rather than one, which allows more material to be taken off one edge than off the other.

Select edge: *Select the edge you want to chamfer.*

Apply distance1 to highlighted face. *Select the face that you want distance1 applied to.*

Flip/<Accept>: *Select option depending on whether the correct face has been highlighted for distance1.*

Distance x Angle   Creates a chamfer defined by a distance and an angle.

Select edge: *Select the edge you want to chamfer.*

Apply distance value to highlighted face. *Select the face that you want distance1 applied to*

Flip/<Accept>: *Select option depending on whether the correct face has been highlighted for distance1.*

Parameters   Defines the specific values of the chamfer.

Distance1   Used for all of the operations; type in the first distance for the chamfer.

Distance2   Used with the Two Distances operation; type in the second distance for the chamfer.

Angle   Used with the Distance x Angle operation; type in the angle for the chamfer.

ADCHAMFER TUTORIAL

This two-part lesson begins with one of the previously created models and modifies it by adding fillets and chamfers to some of the edges. The ADCHAMFER tutorial adds the chamfers, and the ADFILLET tutorial adds the fillets. Unlike the other lessons, you do not need to create sketches or add profiles. To create your feature, simply set the size of your fillet or chamfer and select an edge on the already created model. Upon completion of the two-part tutorial, your modified, extruded part should appear similar to Figure 8–3.

1.   Open your previously created extrusion drawing and save it as fil-chamf.dwg.

Command: **open**

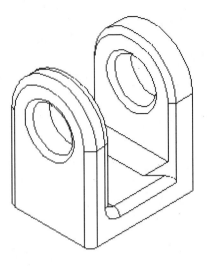

Figure 8-3

Select **extrude1.dwg** in the Open Drawing edit box.

Choose **OK.**

Command: **saveas**

Type in **fil-cham.dwg** in the edit box.

Choose **OK**.

2.   Make sure that your drawing is in Isometric view.

Command: **adpartview**

View option Front/Right/Left/Top/Bottom/Isometric/<Sketch>: **i**

3.   Start with a small chamfer on one of the edges of the part.

Command: **adchamfer**

In the Design Chamfer dialogue box, choose the settings shown in Figure 8–4.

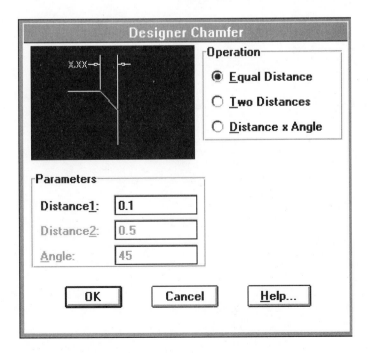

Figure 8-4

Select edge: *Pick P1 of Figure 8–5.*

Select edge: ↵

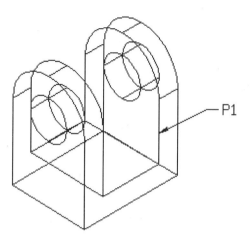

Figure 8–5

4. Next we add another chamfer that combines with the existing one. Depending on the order that fillets and chamfers are applied, the edges form different results. Repeat the chamfer command and choose the dialogue box settings shown in Figure 8–6.

Designer Chamfer

Operation
- ● **E**qual Distance
- ○ **T**wo Distances
- ○ **D**istance x Angle

Parameters

Distance**1**: `0.3`

Distance**2**: `0.5`

Angle: `45`

| OK | Cancel | Help... |

Figure 8–6

Command: ↵

Select edge: *Pick P1 of Figure 8–7.*

Select edge: ↵

The chamfer command can be used to either take edges away or add material as your model should show. It will look like Figure 8–8.

5. Add one last additional chamfer to one of your holes, setting the Designer Chamfer dialogue box as shown in Figure 8–9.

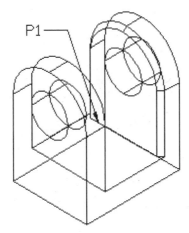

Figure 8-7

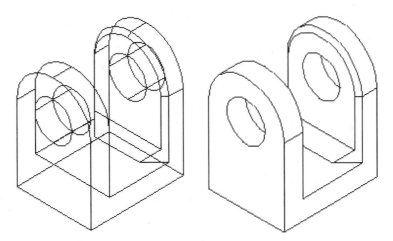

Figure 8-8

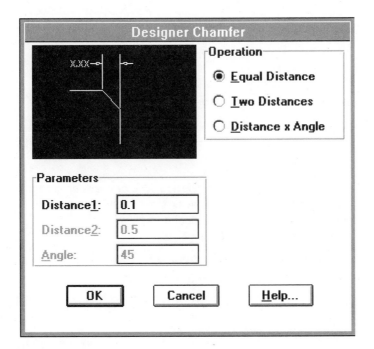

Figure 8-9

Command: ⏎

Select edge: *Pick P1 of Figure 8–10.*

Select edge: ⏎

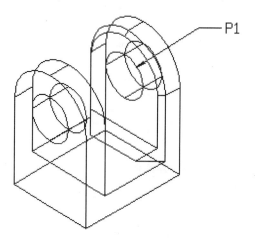

Figure 8-10

Before you begin adding any fillets to your model in the next tutorial, your drawing should look like Figure 8–11. Save your work.

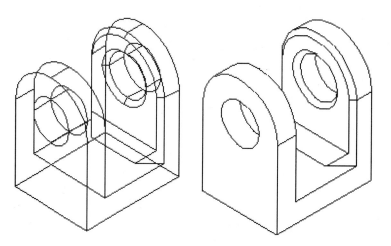

Figure 8-11

ADFILLET

ADFILLET will create a radius along a selected edge or edges of the active part. Radii are applied to most exterior surfaces of molded parts for aesthetic appeal and mold release. Even more important from a design standpoint, radii add structural support to stress-concentrated edges and corners. (See Figure 8–12.)

Command: **adfillet**

Select an edge: *Select an edge you want to apply a fillet to.*

Select an edge: *Select another edge you want to apply a fillet to or press ⏎ to continue.*

Fillet radius <current>: *Type in the radius of your fillet(s).*

As long as the same radius is needed for your fillets, you can select as many edges as you like with one execution of the command. More than one entity may be highlighted

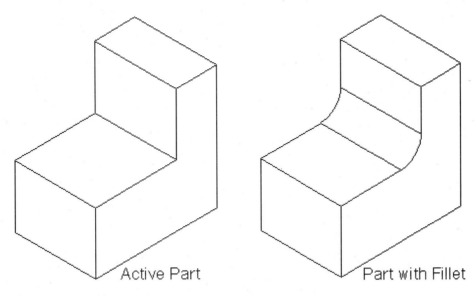

Figure 8-12

when selecting your edge because AutoCAD Designer treats tangent, continuous end-points of joining edges as one edge.

> **Helpful Hint:** Save the creation of any fillets until the very end. This tends to simplify the modeling process.

ADFILLET Tutorial

This tutorial continues the ADCHAMFER tutorial by adding fillets to the active part.

1. The fillet command is even easier than the chamfer command, as it does not have the various dialogue box options. Give it a radius, pick your edge, and your fillet is complete. Create your first fillet on the front side of the hole.

    Command: **adfillet**

    Select edge: *Pick P1 of Figure 8–13.*

    Select edge: ↵

    Fillet radius <current>: **0.1**

    Your part should now look like Figure 8–14.

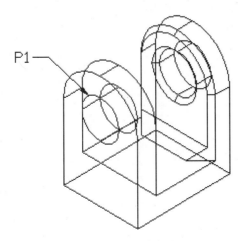

Figure 8-13

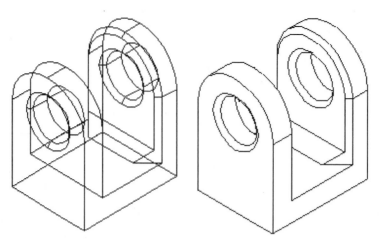

Figure 8-14

2.   Continue to add fillets as described below.

Command: ↵

Select edge: *Pick P1 of Figure 8–15.*

Select edge: ↵

Fillet radius<current>: **0.2**

Before adding your last fillet, make sure your figure has the same edges as Figure 8–16.

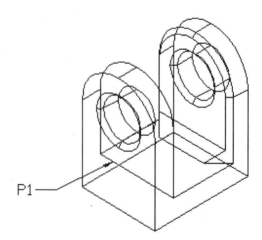

P1—

Figure 8-15

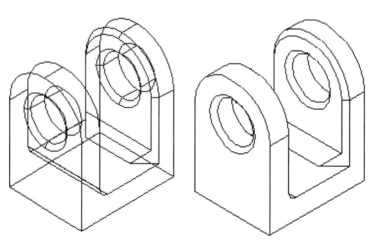

Figure 8-16

3. Add the last fillets.

    Command: ↵

    Select edge: *Pick P1 of Figure 8–17.*

    Select edge: *Pick P2.*

    Fillet radius <current>: **0.15**

You may have difficulty visualizing each edge accurately, but your finished model should resemble Figure 8–18. As you add fillets and chamfers in the future, you may find that there are limits to the sizes and complexities of these features. Experience is the best way to learn the full range of capabilities.

4. Save your work

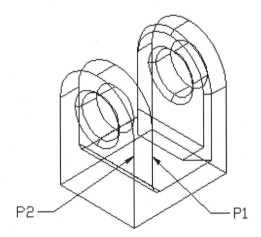

Figure 8-17

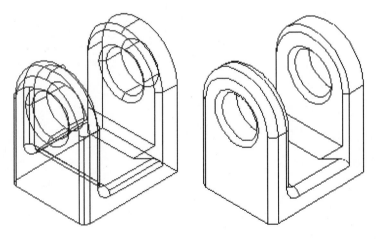

Figure 8-18

REVIEW QUESTIONS

8.1   How many edges can be included in a selection group when using the ADFILLET or ADCHAMFER commands?

8.2   What is the main difference between a fillet and a chamfer?

8.3   Why are radii included in a design?

8.4   Explain the differences between the three operation methods of the ADCHAMFER command.

8.5   When is the best time to add fillets to your model?

CHAPTER EXERCISES

8.1   Add fillets and chamfers to any of the parts you created in previous exercises.

9

EDITING

While you are creating solid parts in AutoCAD Designer, you may need to change them. You may need to extend or shorten a feature, or you may need to remove a feature completely. The commands described in this chapter allow you to modify your model while you are in Part mode.

ADUPDATE

After you change a feature, the **ADUPDATE** command regenerates the active part and drawing and incorporates your modifications.

Command: **adupdate**

The ADUPDATE command displays the changes made to the model by the ADEDITFEAT command (discussed later in this chapter).

The ADUPDATE command is also used when constraining an active sketch. If you are backing up and modifying dimensions, removing constraints, or checking where you are in constraining your sketch, the ADUPDATE command not only updates geometry but also tells you how far you are from attaining a fully constrained sketch.

In Drawing mode, the ADUPDATE command can be used to update both drawing views and the active part.

ADEDITFEAT

The ADEDITFEAT command allows you to modify a selected feature of the active part. Provided the feature was created with a fully constrained sketch, any of its dimensions can be changed to create a modified part (see Figure 9–1).

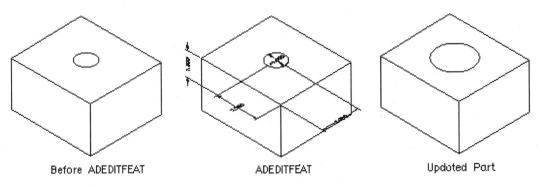

Before ADEDITFEAT   ADEDITFEAT   Updated Part

Figure 9-1

Command: **adeditfeat**

Sketch/<Select feature>: *Select the feature to edit or type s (for sketch).*

Select dimension to change: *Pick an individual dimension to change.*

Dimension value: *Type in the new value for the selected dimension.*

Sketch   The sketch option allows you to change dimensions on the selected feature's sketch. When the feature is selected, AutoCAD Designer will back up the part to the point just before that feature was created. You can use the AutoCAD Designer dimensioning and constraining commands to add, delete, or modify any dimensions or constraints. You cannot change sketch geometry.

If you have a feature that is not fully constrained, you can use the ADEDITFEAT/Sketch option to add the necessary dimensions or constraints to obtain a fully constrained sketch. It is not recommended that you leave your sketches underconstrained, for such sketches may cause editing problems in the future.

When you are finished modifying the sketch, you must use the ADUPDATE command to regenerate the model. AutoCAD Designer will return your model to its previous state, incorporating all modifications.

Select Feature   When you select a feature, AutoCAD Designer allows you to change sketch dimensions only. In order to change sketch constraints or add or delete dimensions/constraints, the sketch option must be used. If the selected feature was made with zero draft, you will not have the option to change the draft; however, if your feature was created with draft, an editable draft dimension appears. Therefore, doublecheck your draft angles when creating features with zero draft because they will be uneditable in the future.

If your selected feature is a hole, the ADHOLE dialogue box will open. Change any dimensions or options as needed and select OK when finished. When all editing is done, use the ADUPDATE command to regenerate your model according to the new dimensions.

ADEDITFEAT TUTORIAL

This tutorial demonstrates the ADEDITFEAT command by opening a model created in a previous tutorial and editing a feature of the part. This tutorial also uses the ADUPDATE command.

1.   Open the drawing of the hand weight you created in Chapter 5.

Command: **open**

Select **revolve2.dwg** in the Open Drawing edit box.

Choose **OK.**

Command: **saveas**

Type in **editing1.dwg** in the edit box.

Choose **OK.**

2.   Change the diameter of the outer cylinders from 3 inches to 4 inches.

Command: **adeditfeat**

Sketch/<Select feature>: *Pick on the front of the cylinder, P1 of Figure 9–2.*

Select dimension to change: *Pick on the 3-inch diameter.*

Dimension value: **4**

3.   Use the ADUPDATE command to visualize the change.

Command: **adupdate**

You should have noticed the outer diameter of the part increase in size. Figure 9–3 shows the new hand weight.

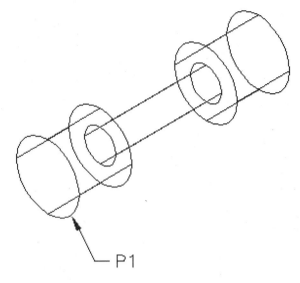

Figure 9-2

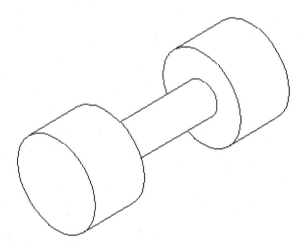

Figure 9-3

ADDELFEAT

Similar to ADEDITFEAT, **ADDELFEAT** allows you to remove a selected feature from the active part. Figure 9–4 shows a hole feature removed from a part using the ADDELFEAT command. While using the ADDELFEAT command you can select a feature for deletion by picking near the middle of that feature. Because more than one feature may be available at the pick location, AutoCAD Designer's picking methods allow you to either accept the highlighted feature or select next to see a different feature.

    Command: **addelfeat**

    Select feature to delete: *Select the feature to be deleted.*

If you see that the selected geometry, after toggling through all the choices, is not what you intended to remove, you can cancel the command.

You will find that many of the features you create are dependent on other features, meaning that they were created by referencing one or more other features to dimensionally constrain the profile. If a feature was used as a reference for creating another feature, it is said to have a **child dependency.** If the selected feature has child dependencies, you will be asked if you want to delete the feature and all its dependencies, which AutoCAD Designer highlights for you. An answer of yes deletes the feature and all child dependencies; an

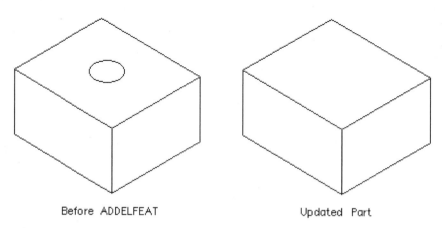

Before ADDELFEAT   Updated Part

Figure 9-4

answer of no cancels the command. Features cannot be deleted without also deleting their dependencies. Therefore, when constraining your profile to the model, try to reference your profile off features that you know will not need to be removed later.

The ADDELFEAT command removes specific features from the active part, but cannot completely remove the active part itself. To completely remove the active part, use the standard AutoCAD ERASE command.

ADDELFEAT TUTORIAL

Instead of editing an existing feature, you will try removing a feature from a part.

1. Open the drawing of the second extruded part you created in Chapter 4.

    Command: **open**

    Select **extrude2.dwg** in the Open Drawing edit box.

    Choose **OK.**

    Command: **saveas**

    Type in **delfeat1.dwg** in the edit box.

    Choose **OK.**

2. Remove the hole from the extruded part.

    Command: **addelfeat**

    Select feature to delete: *Select hole P1 of Figure 9–5.*

    Select feature to delete: ↵

3. Use the ADUPDATE command to show the updated part.

    Command: **adupdate**

    The updated part is shown in Figure 9–6.

4. Save your changed part.

ADMAKEBASE

If you have created a part that you know will not change and you do not want it to change, you can use the **ADMAKEBASE** command. This command still allows you to add various features to your static part, but prevents you from using the ADEDITFEAT or ADDELFEAT commands that modify the part.

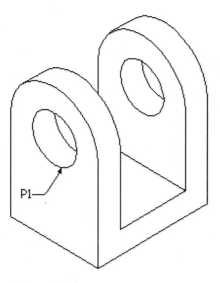

Figure 9-5

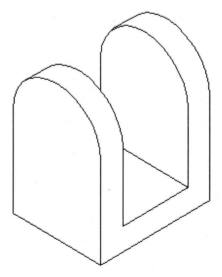

Figure 9-6

Command: **admakebase**

Warning: drawing view information and ability to edit part will be lost.

Create base from highlighted part No/<Yes>: *Choose Yes if the correct part is highlighted.*

Helpful Hint: The ADMAKEBASE command is useful for saving disk space. With this command, AutoCAD Designer compresses part information, resulting in a smaller file size.

If you decide to use the ADMAKEBASE command, remember that you cannot undo this command. Once the part is made static and part data has been compressed, it is no longer recoverable.

ADMAKEBASE TUTORIAL

This tutorial demonstrates the fact that once the ADMAKEBASE command is used to compress a file, the part can no longer be changed. If you are in Windows, use File Manager to look at the file size before and after compression.

1. Open the drawing of the extruded part that you changed in the previous tutorial.

    Command: **open**

    Select **delfeat1.dwg** in the Open Drawing edit box.

    Choose **OK.**

2. Switch to File Manager to look at the file size and switch back after you have recorded the size.

3. Use the ADMAKEBASE command to compress the file.

    Command: **admakebase**

    Warning: drawing view information and ability to edit part will be lost.

    Create base from highlighted part No/<Yes>: **y** ↵

4. Use the ADEDITFEAT command to try editing the part.

    Command: **adeditfeat**

    Sketch/<Select feature>: *Pick anywhere on the part.*

    No editable parameters in base feature.

5. Save the file and switch to File Manager to check the new file size.

REVIEW QUESTIONS

9.1   What is the ADEDITFEAT command used for?

9.2   Are there any limitations to using the ADEDITFEAT command? When can a feature not be changed?

9.3   What is the sketch option used for in the ADEDITFEAT command?

9.4   How is the ADDELFEAT command different from the ADEDITFEAT command?

9.5   What are the results of deleting a feature that has other features dependent on the feature you wish to delete?

9.6   When is the ADUPDATE command used?

CHAPTER EXERCISES

9.1   With the chain link created in the Chapter 6 tutorial, sweep1.dwg, use the ADEDITFEAT command to change the straight portion length from 1.0 to 1.5. Use the ADUPDATE command to see the modified part.

9.2   With the extrude3 drawing file created in the Chapter 4 tutorial and shown in Figure Exer9–2, use the ADEDITFEAT command to change the angle of the workplane that terminates the cylindrical extrusion from 30 degrees to 45 degrees. Use the ADUPDATE command to see the modified part.

9.3   With the drawing created in the Chapter 7 tutorial, hole1.dwg, use the ADDELFEAT command to remove the holes from the part.

9.4   Use the ADEDITFEAT and ADDELFEAT commands to try changing and removing various features of the models created in the exercises for Chapters 4, 5, and 6.

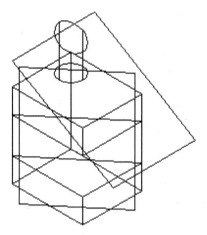

Figure Exer9-2

10

DISPLAY

How you want your model to be displayed will vary depending on what you are doing. AutoCAD Designer gives you some options. ADPARTVIEW automates the process of viewing your model from its various orthographic views and also viewing it from the sketch plane. This method is extremely helpful when you are constructing your three-dimensional model because you can tell AutoCAD Designer the direction from which you want to view your model and then the view point is figured automatically. Another option, **ADISOLINES**, changes the appearance of cylinders in your model. A greater number of isolines makes it easier to visualize a cylindrical model; however, an excessively high isoline value can sometimes add too much definition to a single feature, making it difficult to visualize a combination of features. A value of four or eight usually is sufficient to represent the model clearly without overcrowding the drawing. Lastly, **ADMESH** meshes your model so that the AutoCAD HIDE, SHADE, and RENDER commands can be used.

ADPARTVIEW

ADPARTVIEW allows your model to be viewed from various orientations. You must be in Part mode to use this command.

> Command: **adpartview**

> View option Front/Right/Left/Top/Bottom/Isometric/<Sketch>: *Select a view orientation.*

The first five options correspond to planar views according to AutoCAD's World Coordinate System. These views are defined according to a Front view, which is parallel to the WCS XY plane. The Isometric view is defined by the WCS X, Y, and Z axes, which are all equally distant apart at 120 degrees. You have already practiced switching back and forth between the Sketch view and the Isometric view in previous tutorials. Figure 10–1 gives an example of these view options. The work plane shown in the Isometric view is where the sketch plane is located in this figure.

From the tutorials, you might guess that the Isometric and Sketch views will be the most frequently used orientations. When you view by Sketch, you can see your model from a viewpoint that is perpendicular to your current sketch plane as defined by the User Coordinate System. Sketch viewing simplifies the dimensioning of your profiles/paths, since you are then working with a two-dimensional model rather than a three-dimensional model. In some instances, however, dimensioning a three-dimensional model in the Isometric view may be easier. Once your models become more complicated, the remaining planar views become important for getting the full picture of your model.

ADMESH

ADMESH allows you to toggle between a wire-frame representation and a mesh representation of your model. You will want your part to be in a mesh representation if you wish to use the AutoCAD commands HIDE, SHADE, or RENDER for various surfacing applications. These commands cannot be used if your part is in a standard wire-frame representation. You must be in Part mode to use this command.

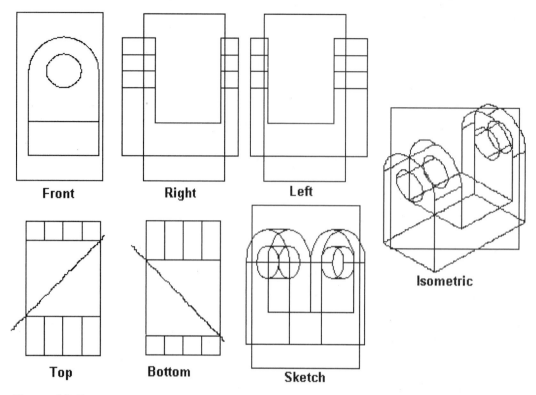

Figure 10-1

Command: **admesh**

OFf/<ON>: *Select an option.*

Select parts to mesh: *Choose any parts that you wish to change the representation on.*

Off   Changes selected parts to a wire-frame representation.

On   Allowable deviation between facets and model <0.1>: *Select a tolerance value for the mesh.*

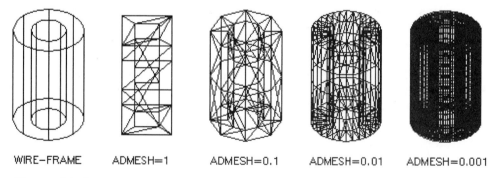

Figure 10-2

Figure 10–2 shows a cylinder at different mesh tolerances. When the mesh tolerance is set to 1, the cylinder appears to be cubical. This is a poor representation of the model. A mesh tolerance value of 0.001 shows a good representation of the model; however, a value this low takes much longer to calculate. Most models can be represented sufficiently with a mesh tolerance value between 0.01 and 0.005. If you need a more accurate representation, you can use 0.001; however, make sure that you have extra time on your hands. We suggest that you don't attempt a tolerance value below 0.001, especially with multiple-feature models. Even with high-speed Pentium computers, AutoCAD Designer requires considerable time to calculate this high-resolution mesh.

It is not recommended that you save your drawings while parts are meshed. First turn off the mesh; then save your work. This sequence will reduce your drawing size and the time needed to save and load your drawing.

Helpful Hint: Do not attempt to use AutoCAD's COPY, ROTATE, SCALE, or MOVE commands on a meshed part. These commands cause the AutoCAD Designer error "Failed to transform part."

ADMESH TUTORIAL

In this tutorial you open one of the extruded features and add different values of mesh to get a feel for the different amounts of resolution. Although the AutoCAD RENDER command is not part of this tutorial, we recommend trying RENDER to apply surfacing once you have a meshed part.

1. Open the extruded part created in Chapter 4.

    Command: **open**

    Select **extrude2.dwg** in the Open Drawing edit box.

    Choose **OK**.

    Command: **saveas**

    Type in **mesh1.dwg** in the edit box.

    Choose **OK**.

2. With the part in an isometric view, use the ADMESH command to mesh the part. Try a value of 0.1 to start.

    Command: **admesh**

    ON/<OFf>: **ON**

    Select parts to mesh.

    Select objects: *Pick anywhere on the model.*

    Allowable deviation between facets and model <current>: **.1**

Your meshed model should appear as shown in Figure 10–3.

3. Turn the mesh off before trying a new value.

    Command: **admesh**

    OFf/<ON>: **OFF**

    Select parts for wire representation.

    Select objects: *Pick anywhere on the model.*

4. Now try a mesh value of 0.001. Notice the increase in complexity of the mesh and also the time difference it takes to mesh the part.

    Command: **admesh**

    ON/<OFf>: **ON**

    Select parts to mesh.

    Select objects: *Pick anywhere on the model.*

    Allowable deviation between facets and model <current>: **.001**

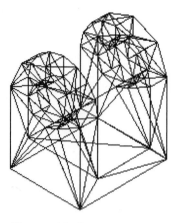

Figure 10-3

Your meshed model should appear as shown in Figure 10–4.

Figure 10-4

5. Save your meshed part.

ADISOLINES

ADISOLINES controls how curved faces will be displayed during a wire-frame representation. ADISOLINES controls two variables: ADISOCYL and ADISONURB.

Command: **adisolines**

Isolines for cones, cylinders, and tori <2>: *Enter a number to control the ADISOCYL variable.*

Isolines for nurbs <0>: *Enter a number to control the ADISONURB variable.*

Figure 10–5 shows a cylinder displayed with different ADISOCYL values, keeping ADISONURB set to 0.

As Figure 10–5 shows, when ADISOCYL is set to 0, the cylinder simply looks like two circles in space. This is not a preferred display method. As the ADISOCYL number is increased, the three-dimensional representation of the model becomes more realistic; however, the complexity of the drawing also increases. It is recommended that the ADISOCYL value be kept at 4 or 8. These values give a good representation of the model without overpowering the drawing. It is also recommended that the ADISONURB value be left at 0. You

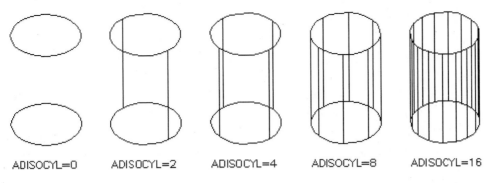

ADISOCYL=0   ADISOCYL=2   ADISOCYL=4   ADISOCYL=8   ADISOCYL=16

Figure 10-5

will rarely encounter Nonuniform rational B splines (**NURBS**) in your models; however, if your models do contain NURBS, then we recommend a value of 4 for ADISONURB. The NURBS value will not affect any of the models created in the tutorials.

Isolines can be used to pick a part; however, you cannot dimension off isolines. If you frequently encounter the error message "Cannot dimension to isolines," temporarily set your ADISOCYL variable to 0. This setting removes all isolines from your display so that you can see exactly what you can dimension from.

When you change the value of ADISOLINES, the change will not take effect until your next update or a forced update, as the following tutorial shows.

ADISOLINES TUTORIAL

This tutorial gives you a chance to try changing your isolines values on a previously created model.

1. Open the hand weight you created in Chapter 5.

   Command: **open**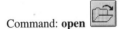

   Select **revolve2.dwg** in the Open Drawing edit box.

   Choose **OK**.

   Your model should resemble that of Figure 10–6. Remember that this drawing was created with isolines set to 4.

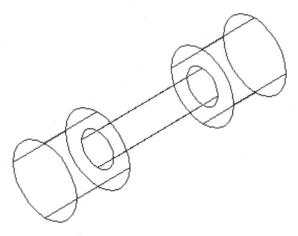

Figure 10-6

2. Change the isoline value to 16.

Command: **adisolines**

Isolines for cones, cylinders, and torii <4>: **16**

Isolines for nurbs<0>: ↵

3. Did you notice a change? You should not have yet! Remember, a change in the isoline or NURB value will not affect the model until the next update. The following prompt forces AutoCAD Designer to perform an update.

Command: (**ad_updatepart 1**)

4. Your updated weight with 16 isolines should now resemble that of Figure 10–7.

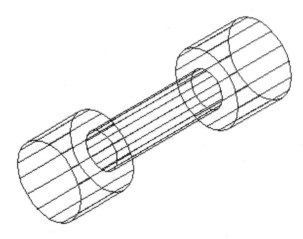

Figure 10-7

REVIEW QUESTIONS

10.1   List the various options of AutoCAD Designer's drawing views. Which two are most commonly used?

10.2   What does the ADMESH command do? When would you want to use it?

10.3   Explain why a smaller mesh value takes longer for AutoCAD Designer to calculate.

10.4   How does the isolines value change the model's display?

10.5   Can isolines be used to place dimensions when referencing a new profile to the model? What will be the result?

CHAPTER EXERCISES

10.1   Use the ADPARTVIEW command to run through the various part views in the extrude3 drawing file you created in the Chapter 4 tutorial.

10.2   Use the ADMESH command to add meshing to the part in the extrude3 drawing file from the previous exercise. Try mesh tolerances of .1, .025, and .003.

10.3   Try changing the isolines display to settings of 2, 8, and 32 in the bat you created in the Chapter 5 tutorial, revolve1.dwg. Use the (AD_UPDATEPART 1) lisp command to force an update on the modified isoline display. Also try changing the NURB value to verify that the part is not affected by this change.

c h a p t e r
11
ORTHO VIEWS

Orthographic views are the two-dimensional views with dimensions and labels that typically are needed for a standard drawing. Once you have created your three-dimensional model in Model space, you can include practically any two-dimensional view that you need to describe your part in Paper space. ADMODE allows you to toggle between Part mode (Model space) where you create three-dimensional parts and Drawing mode (Paper space) where you make two-dimensional drawing views. The explanations of the following view commands describe the process of creating views, toggling between drawing modes, and moving views to or deleting views from Paper space.

ADMODE

The **ADMODE** command allows you to toggle between Part mode and Drawing mode. Most AutoCAD Designer commands can be used only in one of the modes, although there are some commands that can be used in either mode. For example, in order to create a feature you must be in Part mode, but if you wish to edit or delete an orthographic view, you must be in Drawing mode. However, the UPDATE command can be used in either mode. The typical needs for either of the two modes are listed below.

Part Needed to sketch and to create or edit features.

Drawing Needed to create, edit, or remove drawing views.

Command: **admode**

Part/<Drawing>: *Choose the mode needed.*

Helpful Hint: When the ADMODE command is used, the default choice (Part or Drawing) is always the opposite of the currently active mode. Select the default choice by pressing the enter key.

ADMODE TUTORIAL

This tutorial begins the creation of an orthographic drawing. You need to switch into Paper space and insert a title block.

1. Open the extruded part you created in Chapter 4.

    Command: **open**

    Select **extrude2.dwg** in the Open Drawing edit box.

    Choose **OK.**

Command: **saveas**

Type in **ortho1.dwg** in the edit box.

Choose **OK.**

2. Drawing views are always created in Paper space (Drawing mode), so switch now.

Command: **admode**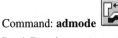

Part/<Drawing>: ↵

3. Set layer 0 as the current layer. Layer 0 is the AutoCAD default layer and the layer on which you will insert a title block.

4. Follow the prompts to insert a standard AutoCAD title block. If you have your own custom title block, you may choose to insert it instead.

Command: **mvsetup**

Align/Create/Scale viewports/Options/Title block/Undo: **T**

Delete objects/Origin/Undo/<Insert title block>: ↵

Add/Delete/Redisplay/<Number of entry to load>: *Choose option 9, ANSI-C Size(in).*

Create a drawing named ansi-c.dwg?<Y>: **no**

Align/Create/Scale viewports/Options/Title block/Undo: ↵

5. Fill in the appropriate information in the title block before saving your work.

ADVIEW

ADVIEW allows you to create two-dimensional as well as Isometric views in Paper space from the solid. View types include Base view, Orthogonal view, Auxiliary view, Isometric view, and Detail view, as shown in Figure 11–1.

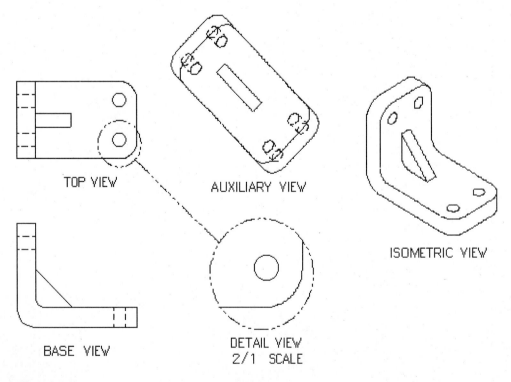

Figure 11-1

Command: **adview**

When the ADVIEW command is used, the Designer Drawing View dialogue box shown in Figure 11–2 appears. Explanations of the various options follow.

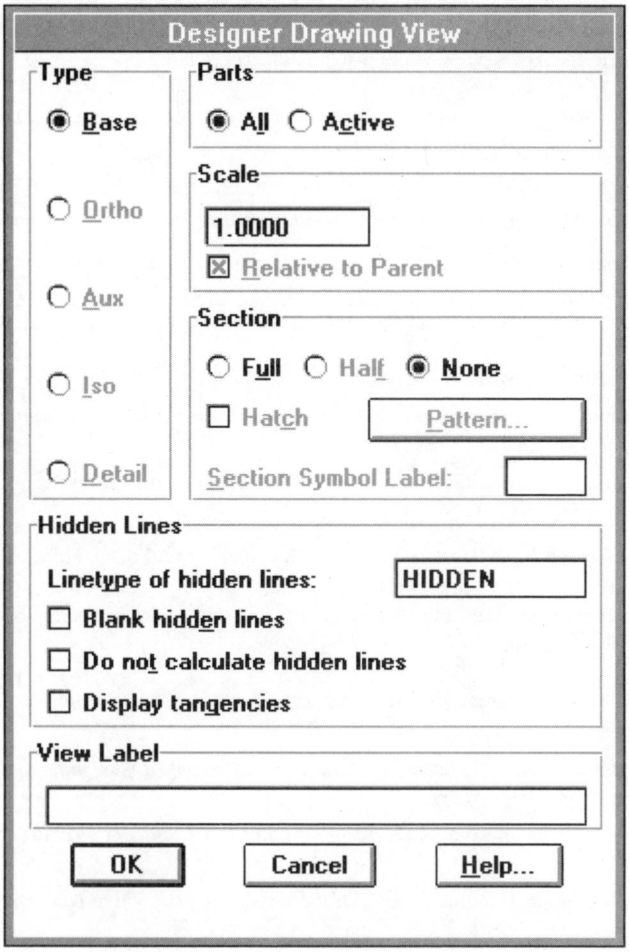

Figure 11–2

Type   Allows you to select a view type.

> **Base**   Base views are two-dimensional views taken from the model and oriented parallel to the chosen work plane or planar face. Unlike Orthogonal views, Base views are not dependent on other views for their attributes. Modifying or deleting other views does not affect the Base view.
>
> > Xy/Yz/Zx/Ucs/<Select work plane or planar face>: *Pick the plane that you want your view to be parallel with.*
> >
> > X/Y/Z/<Select work axis or straight edge>: *Pick an edge that is on your plane.*
> >
> > Rotate/<Accept>: *Choose one based on the orientation of your view.*
>
> After you respond to these command prompts, the screen toggles to Paper space.
>
> View center: *Pick a spot or enter the X and Y coordinates to locate the Base view.*
>
> **Ortho**   Orthographic views are based on an independent parent view in Paper space. Depending on which side of the parent view you pick, AutoCAD Designer creates the new view as an orthographic projection from the parent view. If you consider the parent view the front view, picking above the parent view would result in a top view, picking to the right of the parent view would create a right-side view, etc. AutoCAD Designer automatically orients the view to correspond with the parent view while it maintains proper

scaling, which allows the user to create orthographic views by simply picking and placing.

Aux Auxiliary views are typically face views that cannot be created with an orthographic projection. Instead, auxiliary views are created by selecting an edge in the parent view. The parent view can be the Base view or any other existing view. By selecting to one side or the other, AutoCAD Designer creates a new view perpendicular to that edge. As with Orthographic views, AutoCAD Designer automatically orients the view to correspond with the parent view while it maintains true scaling.

> Select a straight edge in the parent view: *Pick the edge in the parent view that you want the new view projected from.*
>
> Select second point or press ↵ to use the selected edge: *Pick another point if necessary.*
>
> Location for auxiliary view: *Pick on either side of the previously selected edge.*

Iso Creates an isometric view of the part. Isometric views can be shown from four different perspectives depending on which side of the parent view you place them. Unlike Orthographic or Auxiliary views, Isometric views can be moved or scaled independently.

> Select parent view: *Pick the parent view of your part.*
>
> Location for isometric view: *Pick a spot or enter the X and Y coordinates to locate the Isometric view.*
>
> Location for isometric view: *Press ↵ if the view is located where you want it or pick a new location.*

Detail Creates an enlarged scaled view to enhance small details of a part. With Detail view, you can select as small or as large an area of the parent view as you like. The scale of the Detail view is set in the dialogue box, and its positioning is independent of the parent view location.

> Select vertex in parent view for detail center: *Pick on an endpoint of the parent view that you want to be the center of the Detail view.*
>
> Drag rectangle around detail: *Box the area of the parent view that you want to be shown in the Detail view.*
>
> Location for detail point: *Pick a spot or enter the X and Y coordinates to locate the Detail view.*
>
> Location for detail point: *Press ↵ if the view is located where you want it or pick a new location.*

Parts Allows you to choose whether all parts or only the active part will appear in the drawing view.

Scale If you are creating an Isometric or a Detail view, you can set the scale for the drawing view.

Section Cross-sectional views can be made at any point where a work plane is located. When a section view is made, cutting arrows are placed on the parent view to show where the cut was made. The arrows point toward the material of the part that is being maintained. Cross-sections can be created as Base, Orthographic, or Auxiliary views.

> **Full** Creates a full-section view, showing the entire cutting plane.
>
> **Half** Creates a partial-section view, showing the cutting plane at one section and the normal view for the remainder. You need to select a second cutting plane to set the four sections of the part.
>
> **None** No sectional views to be created.
>
> **Hatch** Applies cross-hatching to the sectional view.
>
> **Pattern** Displays the Hatch Option dialogue box where you can set the type of cross-hatching desired.
>
> **Section Symbol Label** Type in the symbol you want to use for the section label.

Hidden Lines Provides options with hidden lines in the view.

> **Linetype of Hidden Lines** Determines linetype for hidden lines.
>
> **Blank Hidden Lines** Removes all hidden lines.

Do Not Calculate   Eliminates hidden lines altogether.

Display Tangencies   Alters the display of tangent edges in the view. See Figure 11–3.

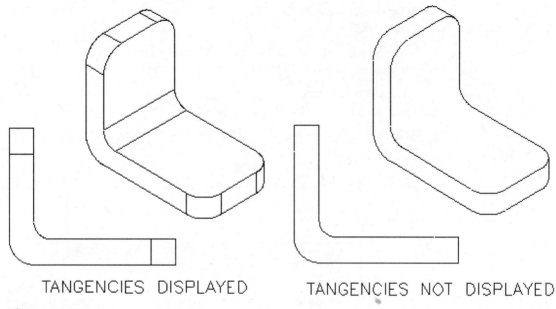

TANGENCIES DISPLAYED   TANGENCIES NOT DISPLAYED

Figure 11-3

View Label   Allows you to enter a label for the new view.

ADVIEW Tutorial

This tutorial continues the creation of an orthographic drawing. When your drawing is finished it should resemble that of Figure 11–4.

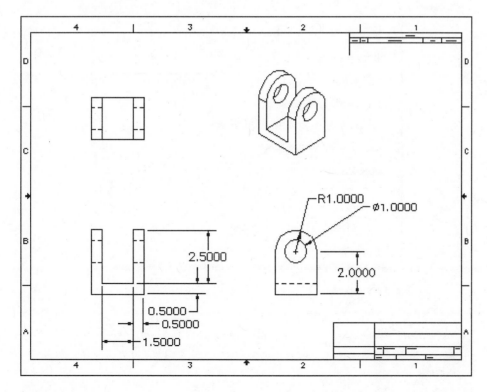

Figure 11-4

1. Open the ortho1.dwg you just created.

    Command: **open**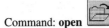

    Select **ortho1.dwg** in the Open Drawing edit box.

    Choose **OK.**

2. Now check to make sure that AutoCAD Designer adds dimensions automatically. You
    can also use the ADSETTINGS command to set this variable.

    Command: **adreusedim**

    New value for ADREUSEDIM (1=yes, 0=no) <1>: **1**

3. Start adding orthographic views. The first view created is always the Base view.

    Command: **adview**

    Accept the default options shown in the Designer Drawing View dialogue box in
    Figure 11–5.

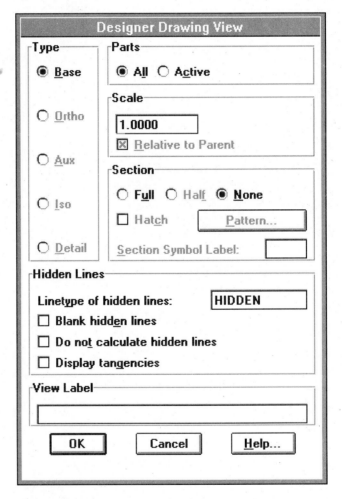

Figure 11–5

Xy/Yz/Zx/Ucs/<Select work plane or planar face>: *Select xy to correspond to the XY WCS.*

X/Y/Z/<Select work axis or straight edge>: *Select x to correspond to the x-axis of the WCS.*

Rotate/<Accept>: ↵

View Center: *Select a location near that in Figure 11–6.*

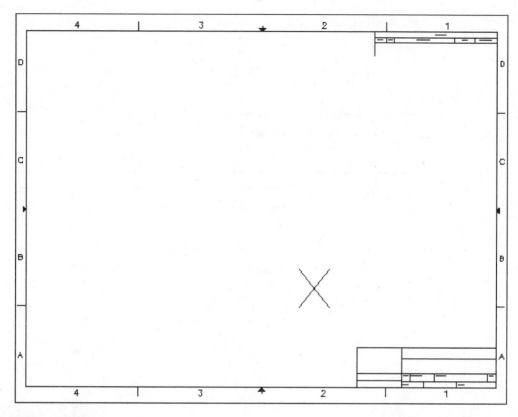

Figure 11-6

Your drawing should resemble that of Figure 11–7. Do not worry if your dimensions are in different locations. You will be moving them in the next chapter.

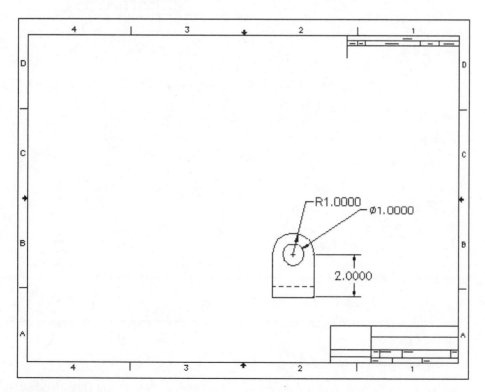

Figure 11-7

4. Create the next view.

    Command: **adview**

    This time select Ortho as the type of view that you want and leave all other options as shown; then select **OK**.

    Select parent view: *Select the view that you just made.*

    Location for orthographic view: *Select a location near that shown in Figure 11–8.*

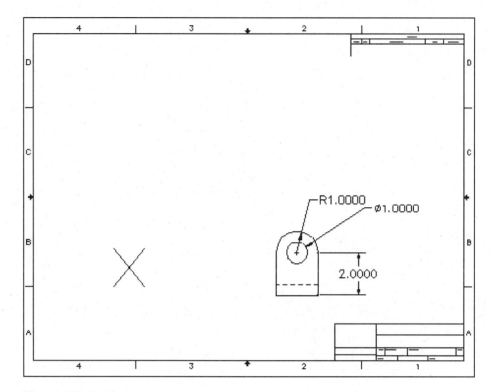

Figure 11-8

    Location for orthographic view: *Once you find an acceptable location, hit enter or the right mouse button to accept it.*

    Your drawing should now resemble that of Figure 11–9.

5. Now add the top view.

    Command: **adview**

    Again, select Ortho as the type of view and leave all other options as shown; then select **OK**.

    Select parent view: *Select the front view (the last view you created).*

    Location for orthographic view: *Select a location near that shown in Figure 11–10.*

    Location for orthographic view: *Once you find an acceptable location, hit enter or the right mouse button to accept it.*

    Your drawing should now resemble that of Figure 11–11.

6. Now that you have three standard orthographic views, include an isometric view in the upper-right corner.

    Command: **adview**

    Select Iso as the view type. Also be sure that Blank hidden lines and Display tangencies are checked. Select **OK**.

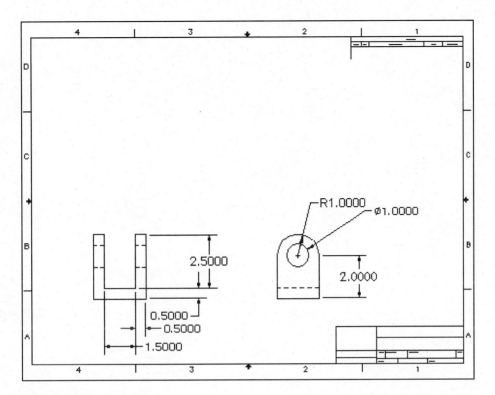

Figure 11-9

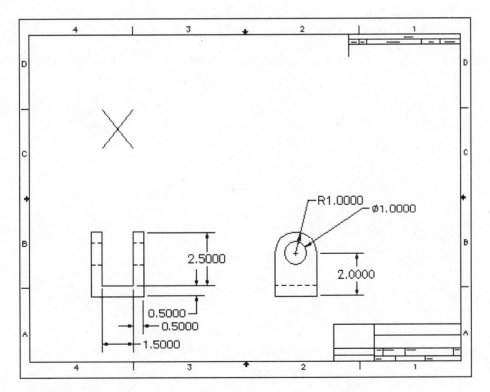

Figure 11-10

Select parent view: *Select the front view.*

Location for isometric view: *Select a point somewhere in the middle of the blank area in the upper-right corner.*

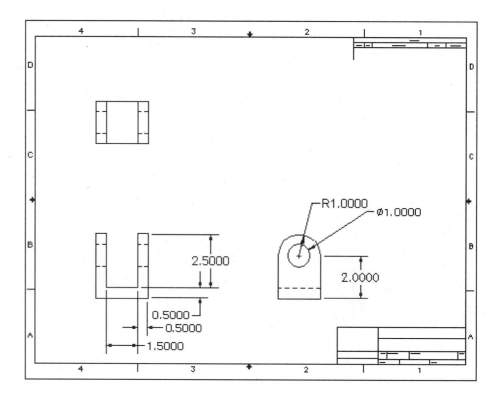

Figure 11-11

Location for isometric view: *Move your view around by selecting different points until the view is where you want to place it.*

Your drawing should now resemble that of Figure 11–12.

7. Save your work.

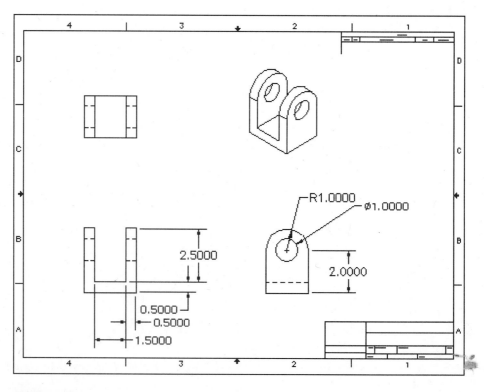

Figure 11-12

ADMOVEVIEW

After creating a few different views in Drawing mode, you may need to reposition some of the views. **ADMOVEVIEW** makes it possible to move a view anywhere on the drawing as long as it is within the restrictions of each view type. Remember, Orthographic views and Auxiliary views need to stay aligned with their parent views.

> Command: **admoveview**
>
> Select view to move: *Pick the view.*
>
> View location: *Pick a spot or enter X and Y coordinates to relocate the view.*

Remember, dependent views move when their parent views move. The ADMOVEVIEW command makes it easy to rearrange the layout of a drawing on a page quickly.

ADMOVEVIEW Tutorial

This tutorial shows how to use the ADMOVEVIEW command to rearrange views.

1. Open the ortho1 drawing that you have been working on.

> Command: **open**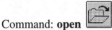
>
> Select **ortho1.dwg** in the Open Drawing edit box.
>
> Choose **OK.**
>
> Command: **saveas**
>
> Type **ortho2.dwg** in the edit box.
>
> Choose **OK.**

2. Practice moving views.

> Command: **admoveview**
>
> Select view to move: *Pick the right view.*
>
> View location: *Select a point approximately 1 inch to the left.*

Notice how all the other views moved accordingly. This is because they are all dependents of the right view, which is the Base view.

3. Try moving the top view to the left.

> Command: **admoveview**
>
> Select view to move: *Pick the top view.*
>
> View location: *Select a point approximately 1 inch to the left.*

Did AutoCAD Designer let you move the view to the left? It shouldn't have because this view is an orthographic view that has to stay aligned with its parent view, the front view.

4. Now try moving the top view up.

> Command: **admoveview**
>
> Select view to move: *Pick the top view.*
>
> View location: *Select a point approximately 1 inch above the top view.*

Did AutoCAD Designer let you move the view this time? We hope so.

5. Save your work.

ADEDITVIEW

While in Drawing mode, **ADEDITVIEW** allows you to modify the scale, associated text, and hidden line display of the selected view. In addition, you can choose new boundaries for a Detail view.

Command: **adeditview**

Select view: *Select a view.*

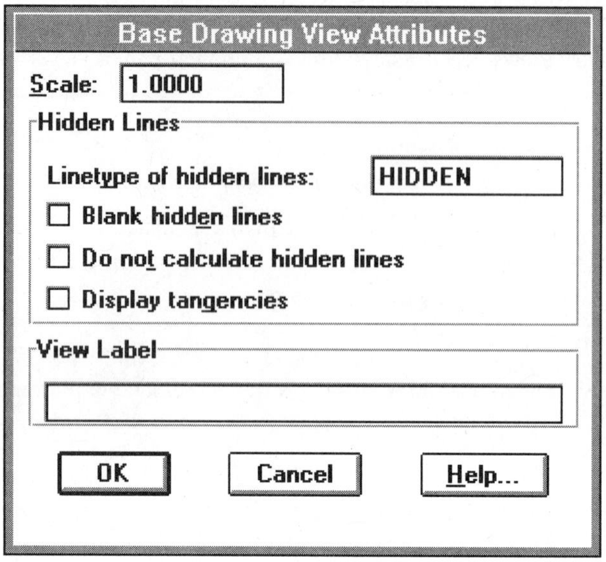

Figure 11-13

Depending on the current drawing view, the Base Drawing View Attributes dialogue box as shown in Figure 11–13 may vary slightly. Also notice that the options in this dialogue box appeared in the ADVIEW dialogue box that you used to create the view.

Scale   Controls the scale of the view.

Hidden Lines   Provides options with hidden lines in the view.

    Linetype of Hidden Lines   Determines linetype for hidden lines.

    Blank Hidden Lines   Removes all hidden lines.

    Do Not Calculate   Eliminates hidden lines altogether.

    Display Tangencies   Alters the display of tangent edges in the view.

View Label   Allows you to enter a label for the new view.

ADEDITVIEW TUTORIAL

This tutorial shows how to use the ADEDITVIEW command to change a view's properties.

1. Open the ortho1 drawing that you have been working on.

    Command: **open**

    Select **ortho1.dwg** in the Open Drawing edit box.

    Choose **OK.**

2. Remove the tangencies from the Isometric view.

    Command: **adeditview**

    Select view: *Select the Isometric view.*

A new dialogue box shows the Isometric view's properties. They represent the same settings as when the view was created. To remove the tangencies simply unmark the Display tangencies box. Your drawing should now resemble that of Figure 11–14.

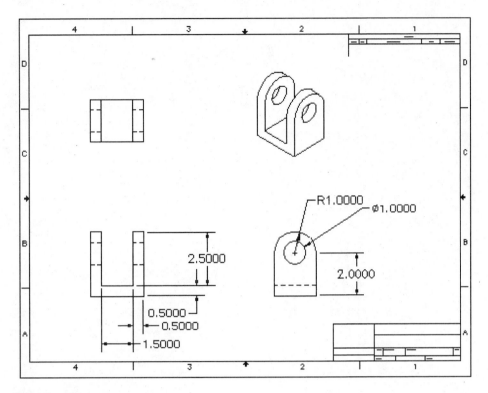

Figure 11-14

ADDELVIEW

When in the drawing mode, **ADDELVIEW** allows you to remove a specified drawing view.

    Command: **addelview**

    Select view to delete: *Pick the view you want to remove.*

If the Drawing view you have selected has dependent views, you have the option of removing these dependents or only the selected parent view.

ADDELVIEW TUTORIAL

This tutorial shows how to use the ADDELVIEW command to remove views.

1. Open the ortho1 drawing that you have been working on.

    Command: **open**

    Select **ortho1.dwg** in the Open Drawing edit box.

    Choose **OK.**

    Command: **saveas**

    Type **ortho3.dwg** in the edit box.

    Choose **OK.**

2. Delete the Isometric view.

    Command: **addelview**

    Select view to delete: *Pick the Isometric view.*

Your drawing should now resemble that of Figure 11–15.

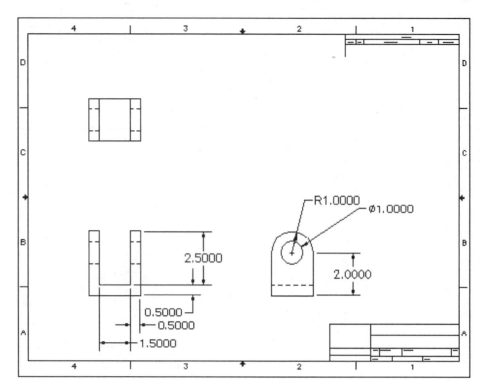

Figure 11-15

3.   Save your work.

REVIEW QUESTIONS

11.1   Describe the function of the ADMODE command.

11.2   Are orthographic views created in Part mode or Drawing mode?

11.3   List and describe the five types of views that can be created with the ADVIEW command.

11.4   How can you make orthographic views of just one part of an assembly drawing?

11.5   When you use the ADMOVEVIEW command to move a view, do dependent views move accordingly or do they stay where they were? Why?

11.6   What kind of view properties can you change with the ADEDITVIEW command?

11.7   When you delete a view with the ADDELVIEW command, are dependent views automatically deleted also?

CHAPTER EXERCISES

11.1–11.12   From the three-dimensional models created in Exercises 4.1 through 4.12, create the three main orthographic views and an isometric view.

11.13–11.24   From the three-dimensional models created in Exercises 4.13 through 4.24, create the orthographic views shown in the exercises. Make sure that your two-dimensional drawings are equivalent to those drawn in the exercises.

11.25   From the model of the retainer clip in Exercise 4.25, create orthographic views including a full-section view through the cylinder.

11.26 From the model of the slide base in Exercise 4.26, create orthographic views including an isometric view.

11.27 From the model of the tool holder created in Exercise 4.28, create orthographic views including an isometric view.

11.28 From the model of the dial bracket created in Exercise 4.29, create orthographic views including an auxiliary view along the angled arm.

11.29 From the fully dimensioned isometric drawing in Figure Exer11–29, use various AutoCAD Designer features to create the release. Create the orthographic views including Detail views of the cuts through the perimeter of the part.

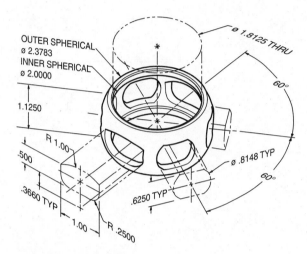

Figure Exer11-29

chapter

12

ORTHO DIMENSIONS

Dimensions on a orthographic drawing convey the exact measurements of your part. Without these dimensions, anyone trying to read your drawing would not be able to determine the size of your part. How can a machinist create your block without knowing if the counterbore is to be 1 inch or ½ inch in diameter? The answer is he or she cannot.

AutoCAD Designer automates the process of adding orthographic dimensions to your drawing. As you create orthographic views, AutoCAD Designer places the appropriate dimensions on the view's features, starting with the Base view. Once these dimensions are placed, you have the option of moving the dimensions from view to view or freezing and thawing dimensions with the **ADFRZDIM** and **ADTHAWDIM** commands. Additional dimensions, for example, reference dimensions and hole notes, can also be added to your orthographic views to further describe a certain feature of your part. You may choose to attach these dimensions to their views by making them annotations, or you may choose to leave them unattached. If you choose not to take advantage of AutoCAD Designer's automatic orthographic dimensioning, you can turn off this option with the ADREUSEDIM command. See Chapter 2 for the use of this command.

ADMOVEDIM

ADMOVEDIM allows dimensions in the AutoCAD Designer Orthographic views to be moved while maintaining their association to the part's geometry. These dimensions can be moved between views or can be redefined on the same view by changing the dimension's attachment points. You must be in Drawing mode to use this command.

> Command: **admovedim**
>
> Reattach/<Move>: *Select a dimension to be moved between views or select r to reattach a dimension on the same view.*
>
> **Reattach**   Select extension line: *Select the dimension extension line to be reattached.*
>
> Select attachment point: *Select a new attachment point for the extension line.*
>
> **Move**   Select view to place the dimension: *Select the view where the dimension will be moved to.*
>
> Location for dimension: *Select the new location for the dimension.*

AutoCAD Designer places dimensions on the first view, which allows the dimension to be displayed according to standard drafting practices. It is common practice for AutoCAD Designer to place many of the dimensions on the Base view and the first Orthographic view created. To make a drawing more understandable, dimensions should be moved and reattached to best define the part. The orthographic drawing in Figure 12–1 illustrates how AutoCAD Designer places the dimensions. The Base view in this drawing is the front view.

Notice that AutoCAD Designer placed all the dimensions on the Base view. This is because the base view is the first view created that allows all dimensions to be displayed according to standard drafting practice. Also notice that the 2.500-dimension extension lines overlap the drawing lines. This is not good drafting practice. It makes this dimension a prime candidate for the reattach option of the ADMOVEDIM command. For illustration purposes the 2.000 horizontal dimension will also be moved to the top view.

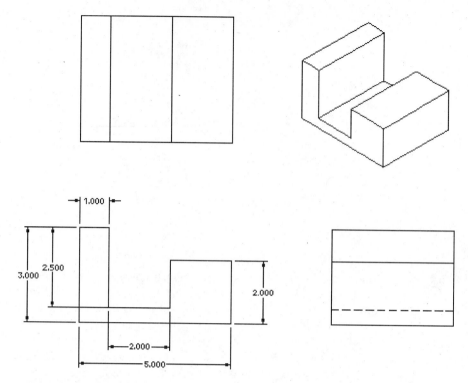

Figure 12-1

The drawing shown in Figure 12–2 is the result of reattaching the 2.500 dimension and moving the 2.000 dimension. You may notice that some dimensions are omitted from this drawing. Any dimensions that are created using AutoCAD Designer's feature commands, such as an extrusion depth, are not added to the orthographic views. These dimensions have to be added as reference dimensions in a process described later in this chapter.

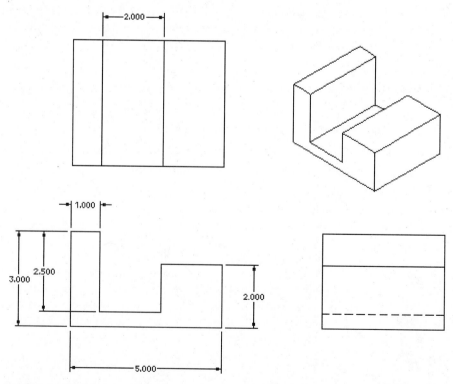

Figure 12-2

Note: When using the reattach option, you must select attachment points that result in the same measured distance as previously defined. For example, the 2.500 vertical dimension shown in Figure 12–1 cannot be reattached to make it the 1.000 dimension shown in Figure 12–3.

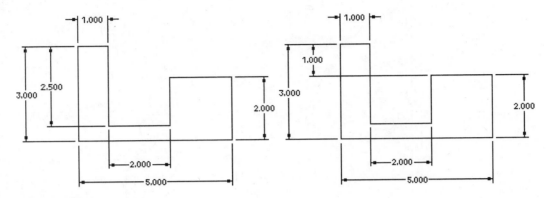

Figure 12-3

ADMOVEDIM TUTORIAL

This tutorial improves the orthographic drawing created in Chapter 11 by moving and reattaching dimensions.

1. Open the orthographic drawing you created in Chapter 11.

   Command: **open**

   Select **ortho1.dwg** in the Open Drawing edit box.

   Choose **OK.**

   Command: **saveas**

   Type **odim1.dwg** in the edit box.

   Choose **OK.**

2. Move the 1.500 dimension on the front view to the top view.

   Command: **admovedim**

   Reattach/<Move>: ↵

   Select dimension to move: *Select the 1.500 dimension on the front view.*

   Select view to place dimension: *Select the top view.*

   Location for dimension: *Select approximately 1 inch above the top view.*

   Your drawing should now resemble that of Figure 12–4.

3. Save your work.

ADFRZDIM

ADFRZDIM allows you to freeze selected dimensions from the orthographic views. Because AutoCAD Designer is a parametric-based program, orthographic dimensions cannot be erased; instead they need to be frozen. One use of freezing dimensions is to dimension a feature differently than AutoCAD Designer dimensioned it. You can freeze the dimension that AutoCAD Designer created automatically and then create a new reference dimension. See **ADREFDIM** later in this chapter. Any dimensions that are frozen using ADFRZDIM remain frozen even when the drawing is updated. You must be in Drawing mode to use this command.

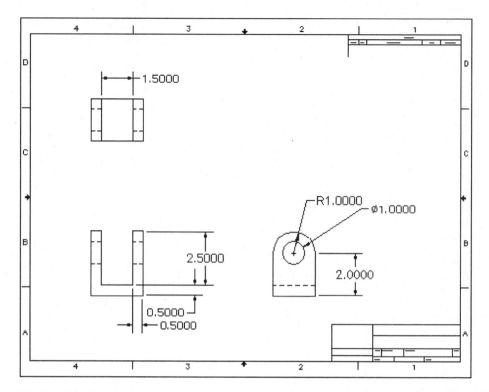

Figure 12-4

Command: **adfrzdim**

Freeze dimensions All/View/<Select>:

All   Freezes all orthographic dimensions.

View   Freezes all orthographic dimensions from a selected view.

Select   Allows for the selection of a dimension to be frozen.

Any dimensions that are frozen with the ADFRZDIM command can be thawed with ADTHAWDIM. See next section.

ADFRZDIM TUTORIAL

This tutorial shows you how to freeze unwanted orthographic dimensions.

1.   Open the orthographic drawing you just modified.

Command: **open**

Select **odim1.dwg** in the Open Drawing edit box.

Choose **OK.**

Command: **saveas**

Type **odim2.dwg** in the edit box.

Choose **OK.**

2.   The 2.500 vertical dimension on the front view is unnecessary. The other dimensions enable a reader to calculate the 2.500 dimension therefore, since the 2.500 vertical dimension is not needed twice, we can freeze it.

Command: **adfrzdim**

Freeze dimensions All/View/<Select>: ↵

Select dimension: *Select the 2.500 dimension from the front view.*

Select dimension: ↵

Your drawing should now resemble that of Figure 12–5.

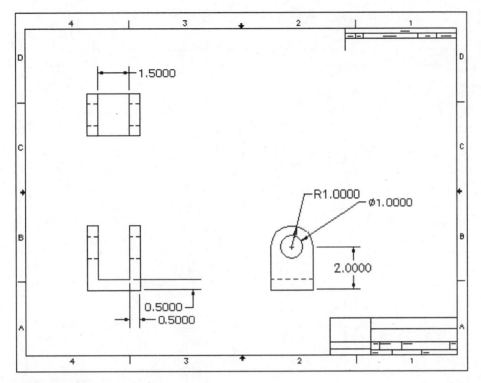

Figure 12-5

3.   Save your work.

ADTHAWDIM

ADTHAWDIM allows you to thaw selected dimensions from the orthographic views that have been frozen using ADFRZDIM. You must be in Drawing mode to use this command.

Command: **adthawdim**

Thaw dimensions View/<All>:

View   Thaws any frozen dimensions from a selected view.

All   Thaws all frozen dimensions.

ADTHAWDIM Tutorial

This tutorial shows you how to thaw frozen orthographic dimensions.

1.   Open the orthographic drawing you just finished.

Command: **open**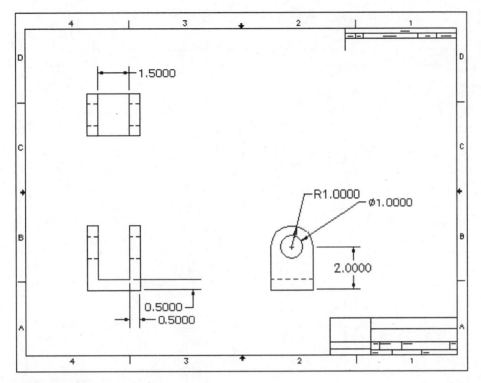

Select **odim2.dwg** in the Open Drawing edit box.

Choose **OK.**

Command: **saveas**

Type **odim3.dwg** in the edit box.

Choose **OK.**

2.   Thaw the dimension you froze in the previous tutorial.

Command: **adthawdim**

Thaw dimensions View/<All>: ↵

Your drawing should resemble that of Figure 12–6.

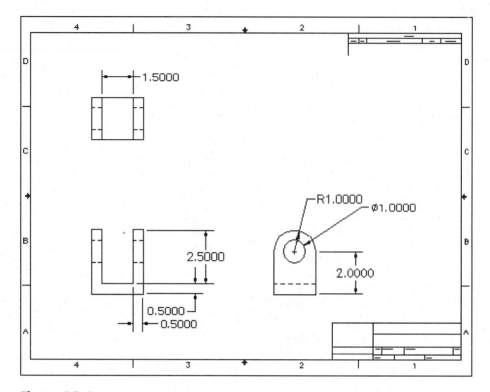

Figure 12-6

3.   Save your work.

ADREFDIM

ADREFDIM allows you to create a reference dimension on the orthographic views. You can use reference dimensions to add some of the dimensions that AutoCAD Designer did not automatically place for you, or you may choose to dimension your whole part using reference dimensions with the ADREUSEDIM option turned off. You must be in Drawing mode to use this command.

Command: **adrefdim**

Select first item: *Select an item to dimension.*

Select second item or place dimension: *Select a second item or select a point to place the dimension.*

Undo/Hor/Ver/Align/Par/Ref/Basic/Placement point: *Enter an option or a new value for the dimension.*

Undo   Cancels the ADREFDIM command.

Hor   Restricts the dimension to be horizontal.

Ver   Restricts the dimension to be vertical.

Align   Restricts the dimension to be aligned.

Par   Restricts the dimension to be parallel.

Ref   Creates a reference dimension.

Basic   Creates a basic dimension that has a rectangle around the dimension value.

Placement Point   Selects a point to move the created dimension to.

Use a combination of parametric dimensions and reference dimensions to fully dimension your drawing so that it may be interpreted by another user. ADREFDIM is similar to ADPARDIM. Refer to Chapter 3 for detailed explanations of the dimensioning options.

Helpful Hint: AutoCAD Designer does not automatically place Z coordinate dimensions, for example, extrusion depths, on the orthographic views. These types of dimensions make good reference dimensions.

The ADDIMATT command, explained in Chapter 14, controls the style of the reference dimensions.

ADREFDIM TUTORIAL

This tutorial adds a reference dimension to the orthographic drawing.

1. Open the orthographic drawing odim2.

    Command: **open**

    Select **odim2.dwg** in the Open Drawing edit box.

    Choose **OK.**

    Command: **saveas**

    Type **odim4.dwg** in the edit box.

    Choose **OK.**

2. Add a reference dimension that represents the overall length of the part.

    Command: **adrefdim**

    Select first item: *Select P1 of Figure 12–7.*

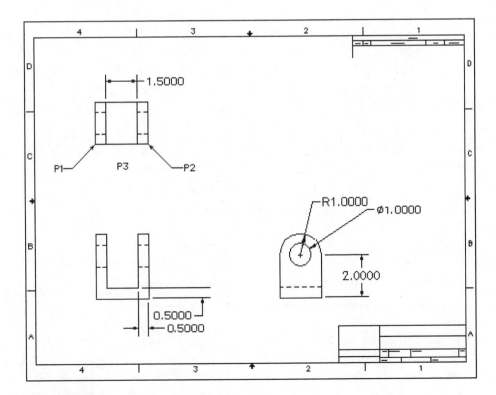

Figure 12-7

Select second item or place dimension: *Select P2.*

Specify dimension placement: *Select P3.*

Undo/Hor/Ver/Align/Par/Ref/Basic/Placement point: ↵ *to accept the point.*

Select first item: ↵

Your drawing should now resemble that of Figure 12–8.

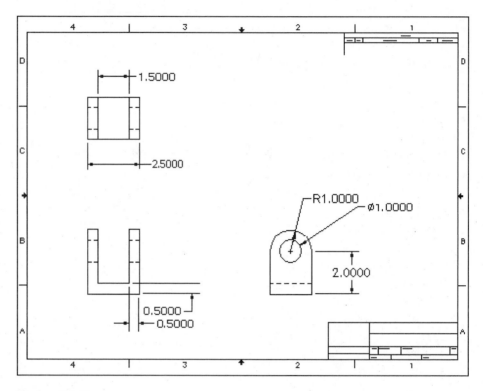

Figure 12-8

3.   Save your work.

ADDELREF

ADDELREF allows you to delete reference dimensions from the orthographic views. Parametric dimensions cannot be deleted using this command; you must freeze them using the ADFRZDIM command. ADDELREF works only in Drawing mode.

Command: **addelref**

Select view dimension: *Select a reference dimension to delete.*

ADDELREF TUTORIAL

This tutorial deletes the reference dimension that you just created..

1.   Open the orthographic drawing odim4.

Command: **open**

Select **odim4.dwg** in the Open Drawing edit box.

Choose **OK.**

Command: **saveas**

Type **odim5.dwg** in the edit box.

Choose **OK.**

2. Delete the reference dimension that you just created.

Command: **addelref**

Select view dimension: *Select the 2.500 reference dimension from the top view.*

Your drawing should now resemble that of Figure 12–9.

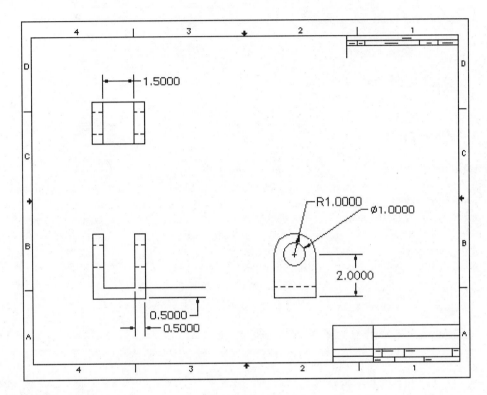

Figure 12-9

3. Save your work.

ADHOLENOTE

ADHOLENOTE automates the creation of a leader with the diameter depth and angle information listed for a selected hole in your drawing. You must be in Drawing mode to use this command.

Command: **adholenote**

Select arc or circle of hole feature: *Select an arc or circle from the hole that you wish to annotate. Do not select the hole's isolines.*

Location for the hole note: *Select a location where you want the hole note to appear.*

An example of a hole note is shown in Figure 12–10. Notice how all the relevant information that was used to create the hole is shown. Unfortunately, hole notes are not considered parametric dimensions. If you wish to change the dimensions of the hole, you must switch to Part mode and use the ADEDITFEAT command on the hole (see Chapter 9). Then, when you perform the needed ADUPDATE, after using ADEDITFEAT, the hole note will be updated automatically.

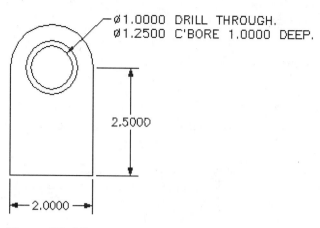

Figure 12-10

ADANNOTE

ADANNOTE allows you to create annotations that are parametrically bound to your drawing views. Once annotations are created, you can move, delete, add to, and remove from them. Any AutoCAD entity can be established as an annotation bound to a particular orthographic view. One time to use ADANNOTE is when adding geometric tolerance notes to a drawing. Then, if you later use the ADMOVEVIEW command to move your orthographic views, any annotations created to these views will move accordingly. You must be in Drawing mode to use this command.

Command: **adannote**

Create/Delete/Move/Add/Remove: *Select an option from the list.*

Create   Select entities to make an annotation.

Select objects: *Select as many two-dimensional AutoCAD entities as you want to group into one annotation attached to one particular view.*

Locate point to attach annotation. *Pick a point on the part's geometry within the view you want to see the annotation connected to.*

Leader start point: *Pick any point on your drawing to define the starting point of the leader.*

Leader end point: *Pick any point on your drawing to define the endpoint of the leader.*

Next leader vertex: *If so desired, continue entering vertex points. ↵ stops this process.*

Helpful Hint: When grouping annotations, it is not recommended that you select an entity that is located on one view to become an annotation attached to a different view. This may cause unexpected results when using the ADMOVEVIEW command, depending on whether the views are dependent upon each other.

The location point used to attach the entities to a view may not be a silhouette edge. You must select a defined AutoCAD Designer vertex on the part geometry, such as an endpoint of a line or the center of an arc/circle. This restriction does not apply to leader points. They may be defined anywhere on the drawing. If no leader is desired simply press enter when prompted for a leader endpoint.

Delete   Select annotations by selecting any of its entities: *Pick anywhere on an annotation to select it for deletion.*

When you use the delete option of ADANNOTE, all entities of the selected annotation are erased from your drawing and removed from the AutoCAD database. If you do not wish to erase the entities, use the remove option instead of the delete option.

Move   Select annotations by selecting any of its entities: *Pick anywhere on an annotation to select it for moving.*

Note location: *Select a new location for the annotation.*

When moving an annotation, the start point of the annotation's leader remains stationary. Only the annotation and the leader lines will be moved.

Add   Select annotations by selecting any of its entities: *Pick an annotation that you want to add entities to.*

Select entities to add to annotation.

Select objects: *Select as many two-dimensional AutoCAD entities as you want to add to the chosen annotation.*

The add option of ADANNOTE is useful when entities have been added to your drawing after annotations have already been established. It is recommended that you maintain only one annotation per orthographic view. This practice helps maintain drawing simplicity.

Remove   Select items to remove from annotation

Select objects: *Select as many two-dimensional AutoCAD entities as you want to remove from the chosen annotation.*

This option removes selected entities from the annotation. Remove's advantage over delete is that after the entities have been removed, they are not erased from your drawing or removed from the AutoCAD database.

ADMOVELDR

ADMOVELDR allows you to relocate the start point of an annotation leader. This is the one thing that the move option of ADANNOTE does not allow you to do. You must be in Drawing mode to use this command.

Command: **admoveldr**

Select a leader entity: *Select the leader you wish to relocate.*

Leader start point: *Select a new start point for the leader.*

REVIEW QUESTIONS

12.1   When creating orthographic views with AutoCAD Designer's ADVIEW command, is every dimension automatically added? If no, explain which types of dimensions are not included.

12.2   When you move a dimension with the ADMOVEDIM command, is that dimension's associativity maintained?

12.3   When do you need to use the ADFRZDIM command? What does this command do?

12.4   Which other AutoCAD Designer command is similar to ADREFDIM?

12.5   Can parametric dimensions be deleted with the ADDELREF command? If no, what command is needed to do this?

12.6   What does the ADHOLENOTE command do?

12.7   In what ways are the dimensions created with ADHOLENOTE parametric, and in what way are they not?

12.8   Define an annotation.

12.9   What does the ADMOVELDR command allow you to do that ADANNOTE does not?

CHAPTER EXERCISES

12.1–12.12   From the orthographic drawings created in Exercises 11.1 through 11.12, add any necessary reference dimensions or annotations to create fully dimensioned drawings.

12.13   Open your hole1 drawing from Chapter 7 and create a fully dimensioned orthographic drawing with a title block. Use the ADHOLENOTE command to add dimensions to the holes.

12.14   From the protector created in Exercise 7.2, create a fully dimensioned orthographic drawing that includes a title block and hole notes.

13

PARTS

This short chapter describes three commands that allow you to see, switch to, and create new parts. Used in Part mode, these commands are generally for multiple-part drawings.

ADNEWPART

The **ADNEWPART** command allows you to begin a new part of a multiple-part drawing.

Command: **adnewpart**

When creating your first part, you do not need to use the ADNEWPART command. Use this command when you already have existing parts and wish to begin a new sketch for an additional part.

ADNEWPART TUTORIAL

This tutorial gives you the first look at a multiple-part drawing. You will use the bat created in Chapter 5 and add a ball to go along with it.

1. Open the drawing file containing the bat created in Chapter 5.

    Command: **open**

    Select **revolve1.dwg** in the Open Drawing edit box.

    Choose **OK.**

    Command: **saveas**

    Type in **part1.dwg** in the edit box.

    Choose **OK.**

2. Use the ADNEWPART command to begin a new model.

    Command: **adnewpart**

3. Use the techniques you learned in Chapter 5 to create a 1.5-inch-diameter ball somewhere near the bat. Your final two-part drawing should look similar to Figure 13–1.

4. Use the ADEDITFEAT command to try changing the overall length of the bat from 13 inches to 15 inches. Since the ball is the new active part, you will not be able to modify the bat without switching the active part. The ADACT-PART command follows this tutorial.

5. Save your drawing.

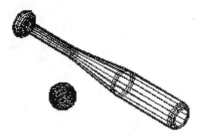

Figure 13-1

ADACTPART

The **ADACTPART** command allows you to switch the active part of a multiple-part drawing.

> Command: **adactpart**
>
> Select part: *Select the part you wish to be active.*

ADACTPART TUTORIAL

This tutorial shows you how to toggle between active parts of a multiple-part drawing. You will use the two-part drawing created in the previous tutorial.

1. Open the two-part drawing file you created in the last tutorial.

    Command: **open**

    Select **part1.dwg** in the Open Drawing edit box.

    Choose **OK.**

2. Since the ball is currently the active part, use the ADACTPART command to switch the active part.

    Command: **adactpart**

    Select part: *Pick the bat.*

3. Now try using the ADEDITFEAT command to change the overall length of the bat from 13 inches to 15 inches. After the ADUPDATE command, your new bat and ball should resemble Figure 13–2.

Figure 13-2

4. Save your work.

ADSHOWACT

When switching active parts in a multiple-part drawing, you can use the **ADSHOWACT** command to highlight the active part, sketch, or sketch plane.

Command: **adshowact**

PArt/Sketch plane/<PRofile>: *Select the option you want to show.*

Part   Highlights the active part.

Sketch Plane   Highlights the active sketch plane.

Profile   Highlights the active sketch.

Keep in mind that you need to be working on an active part or sketch to use most of the AutoCAD Designer commands.

ADSHOWACT TUTORIAL

This tutorial gives you an idea of how the highlighted active parts will appear when you use the ADSHOWACT command.

1. Open the two-part drawing file you recently created in the previous tutorial.

    Command: **open**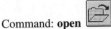
    Select **part1.dwg** in the Open Drawing edit box.
    Choose **OK.**

2. Use the ADSHOWACT command to show the active part. Your highlighted drawing should be similar to Figure 13–3.

    Command: **adshowact**
    PArt/Sketch plane/<PRofile>: **pa**

Figure 13-3

REVIEW QUESTIONS

14.1   When is the ADNEWPART command used? Does it need to be used before creating the first part of a drawing?

14.2   What is the ADACTPART command used for?

14.3   What are the viewing options of the ADSHOWACT command?

CHAPTER EXERCISES

14.1   With the part1 drawing file, first use the ADSHOWACT command to check to see which part is active. Second, if the ball is not the active part, use the ADACTPART command to make it active. Use the ADEDITFEAT command to change the diameter of the ball from 1.5 inches to 2 inches.

14.2   With the part1 drawing file, add an additional part to the drawing. Create a simple extrusion shaped like the home plate of a baseball field.

chapter

14

UTILITIES

The AutoCAD Designer utility commands allow you to set standard variables for your drawing and obtain valuable information about your model. For example, AutoCAD Designer's **ADMASSPROP** command calculates the volume, mass, and center of gravity of your model. This information may be vital to a three-dimensional model. How heavy will the part be when the customer picks it up? How large is the part? Before AutoCAD Designer, engineers had to hand calculate the answers to these questions. Now AutoCAD Designer does the calculations for them. **ADLIST** provides information about features, parts, and drawing views of the model. AutoCAD Designer system variables such as angular tolerance, projection type, and dimension text height are set using ADSETTINGS and ADDIMATT.

ADMASSPROP

ADMASSPROP calculates and displays the three-dimesional properties of your model, including volume, mass, and center of gravity. These values depend on the density that you enter for your model. ADMASSPROP can be used on one part or multiple parts, and the Designer Mass Properties dialogue box appears depending on how many parts you select. You must be in Part mode to use this command.

Command: **admassprop**

All/Select/<ACtive>: *Select an option.*

All   Calculates the mass properties for all parts.

Select   Allows you to select one or more parts for which the mass properties will be calculated.

Active   Calculates the mass properties for the active part only.

When you select only one part, the Designer Mass Properties dialogue box shown in Figure 14–1 appears. With just one part selected, AutoCAD Designer also calculates the part's moments of inertia, principal moments, and radii of gyration along with other information. The density value assigned to the part can be changed here. Use a density value that has units of measurement that are the same as your drawing. For example, if your part is drawn in inches and you want the mass in pounds, enter a density value that has pounds per cubic inch as its units. If selected, the Write to File box writes the mass property information to the specified file name.

When you select multiple parts, the dialogue box shown in Figure 14–2 appears. You can assign different density values to different parts by selecting the desired part and entering a density. If you select Apply to All, the specified density will be applied to all the parts.

ADMASSPROP TUTORIAL

This tutorial shows you the usefulness of the ADMASSPROP command by using the hand weight solid model you created in Chapter 5. You can use the density of various materials to get corresponding weight values for the hand weight.

183

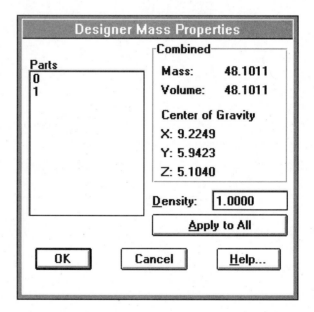

Figure 14–1

Figure 14–2

1. Open the model of the hand weight you created in Chapter 5.

    Command: **open**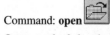

    Open revolve2.dwg by selecting the drive and directory of the file and then selecting the file.

    Choose **OK.**

2. Use the ADMASSPROP command to enter a density for the hand weight to get a mass value.

   Command: **admassprop**

   All/Select/<ACtive>: **ac**

   The one-part Designer Mass Properties dialogue box shown in Figure 14–3 will appear.

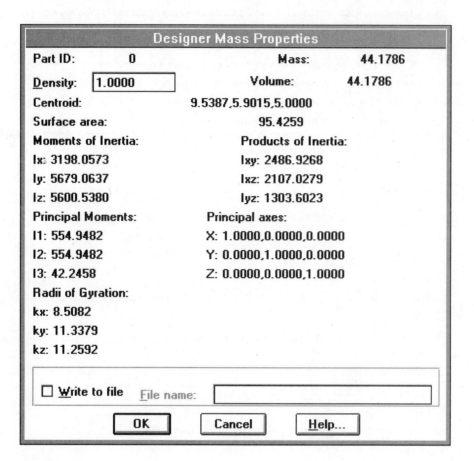

Figure 14–3

3. Start by trying a gray, cast iron material with a density of 0.258 lbm/in^3. At the prompt for density, type **.258** and hit return. A new mass of 11.3981 should be displayed immediately.

4. Now try entering the density of a lightweight material such as an aluminum alloy. At the density prompt, type **.101.** A new mass value of 4.4620 should be displayed immediately.

ADLIST

ADLIST provides information about the features, parts, and views in your drawing.

Command: **adlist**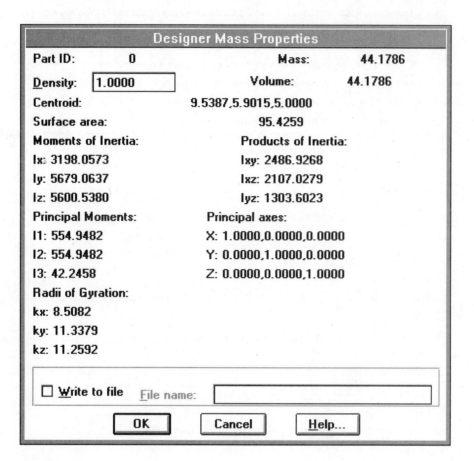

Feature/Part/<View>: *Pick an option.*

Feature   Lists information about any parental dependencies, children, and general feature information. You must be in Part mode to use the feature option.

Select features: *Select one or more features that you wish to obtain information about.*

Children/Parents/<List>: *Select an option.*

> **Children**   Displays all the features that are dependent on the previously selected feature(s).
>
> **Parents**   Displays the parent of the selected feature(s).
>
> **List**   Displays a list of the selected feature's properties.

Part   Displays a list of the selected part's feature information and its ID. You must be in Part mode to use the part option.

All/Select/<ACtive>: *Select an option.*

> **All**   Displays information for every part in your current drawing.
>
> **Select**   Allows you to select parts for which you want to display information.
>
> **Active**   Displays information only on the active part.

View   Lists information about a selected view including its type, ID, center point, name of its layers, number of dependent views, and number of parts represented by the view. You must be in Drawing mode to use this command.

ADLIST TUTORIAL

This tutorial gives an example of one of the ADLIST command's many uses.

1. Once again, open the model of the hand weight you created in Chapter 5.

    Command: **open**

    Open revolve2.dwg by selecting the drive and directory of the file and then selecting the file. Choose **OK.**

2. Use the ADLIST command to display the properties of a feature selected on the hand weight.

    Command: **adlist**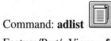

    Feature/Part/<View>: **f**

    Select features: *Pick on the end of the weight, P1 of Figure 14–4.*

    Children/Parents/<List>: **l**

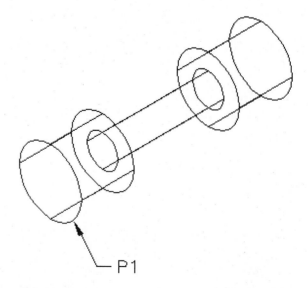

Figure 14-4

The selected features' properties will appear as shown in Figure 14–5.

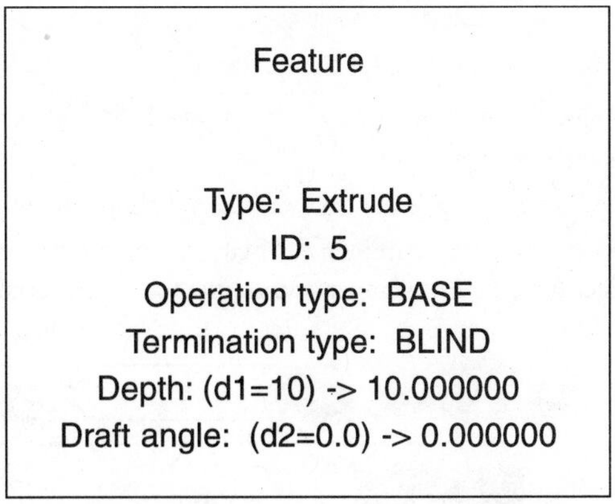

```
                        Feature


                  Type:  Extrude
                     ID:  5
                  Operation type:  BASE
                  Termination type:  BLIND
                  Depth: (d1=10) -> 10.000000
                  Draft angle:  (d2=0.0) -> 0.000000
```

Figure 14-5

ADDIMATT

ADDIMATT allows you to change the properties of drawing view dimensions. The Designer Dimesion Options dialogue box shown in Figure 14–6 appears when this command is utilized.

Command: **addimatt**

Select dimension to edit: *Pick a dimension for property editing.*

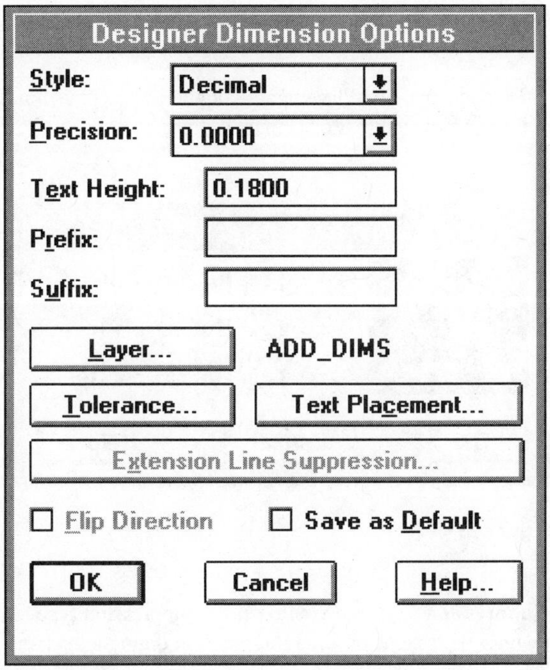

Figure 14-6

Style   Selects the type of units.

    Scientific   2.31E+012

    Decimal   23.10

    Engineering   1'-9.10"

    Architectural   1'-9 1/10"

    Fractional   23 1/10

Precision   Sets the number of decimal places.

Text Height   Controls the text height for the dimensions.

Prefix   Determines the dimension prefix.

Suffix   Determines the dimension suffix.

Layer   Displays the Layer dialogue box so that you can choose a layer for dimesions.

Tolerance   Displays the Dimension Tolerances dialogue box as shown in Figure 14–7. From this box you can select the type of tolerance and set the tolerance variables.

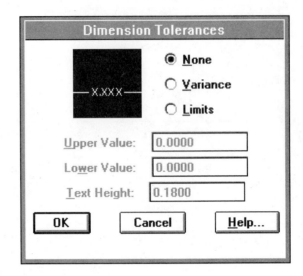

Figure 14–7

Text Placement   Displays the Text Placement dialogue box as shown in Figure 14–8. From this box you can set the arrow and text placement options.

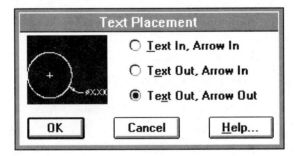

Figure 14–8

Extension Line Suppression   Allows you to set the suppression type to be used on the dimensions from within the Extension Line Suppression dialogue box shown in Figure 14–9.

Flip Direction   Flips the dimension and text location.

Save as Default   Saves your current settings so that they are applied to future dimensions.

ADVER

ADVER displays the version number of the AutoCAD Designer software that you are running.

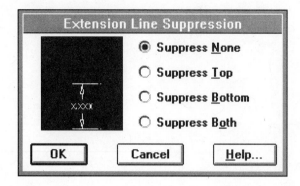

Figure 14-9

Command: **adver**

ADVER = "R1.2" (read only)

REVIEW QUESTIONS

14.1   Explain the use of the ADMASSPROP command.

14.2   Give some specific applications for the ADMASSPROP command.

14.3   When using the ADMASSPROP command, what additional properties are given when only one part is selected versus more than one?

14.4   What types of information does the ADLIST command provide?

14.5   What are the differences between the three options of the ADLIST command?

14.6   Explain the use of the ADDIMATT command.

14.7   What are the different dimensioning styles that can be selected with the ADDIMATT command? Give an example of each style.

14.8   What tolerancing options are available from the ADDIMATT command?

14.9   What does the ADVER command display?

CHAPTER EXERCISES

14.1   Use the ADVER command to check what version of AutoCAD Designer you are using.

14.2   Using stainless steel with a density of 0.27lb/in^3, determine the weight of the chain link created in Chapter 6.

14.3   Determine the volume of the ball created in Chapter 13.

14.4   Using the extrude1 block created in Chapter 4, display a list of the part's feature information and ID.

14.5   Use the ADLIST command to determine the children and parent features of the extrude2 model created in Chapter 4.

14.6   With the odim1 drawing created in Chapter 12, pick any two dimensions and change the ADDIMATT settings to the following: Precision = 0.0; Text Height = 0.156; Tolerance: Variance, Upper Value = 0.1, Lower Value = 0.1; and Text Placement: Text In, No Arrow.

15

TRANSFER

The transfer commands are an important aspect of AutoCAD Designer. These commands allow you to share your AutoCAD Designer model with other users for various applications. Communicating your ideas with others is an important part of the design process. You can use the **ADPARTIN** command to insert your drawing into a three-dimensional model assembly. If your application calls for an actual prototype, the **ADSATOUT** command is quite handy. After a model has been saved in the .sat format, it can be translated into a StereoLithography file for rapid prototyping. Sometimes further surfacing, beyond what AutoCAD Designer can provide, is needed. You can use the **ADASFCONV** command to translate your AutoCAD Designer model into a surface model that can be read by AutoSurf®. You must be in Part mode to use any of the AutoCAD Designer transfer commands.

ADPARTOUT

ADPARTOUT writes AutoCAD Designer parts into separate .dwg files. Any parts that are written by ADPARTOUT are fully editable and are in no way linked to the original file. One use of this command is to write parts that belong to an assembly drawing to separate files so that individual drawings may be made from them. This command is very similar to the AutoCAD WBLOCK command; however, ADPARTOUT saves AutoCAD Designer data only.

> **Helpful Hint:** Do not use the AutoCAD WBLOCK command when exporting AutoCAD Designer parts. AutoCAD Designer data will not be included in the block.

Command: **adpartout**
Enter file name: *Enter a file name.*
Select insert point: *Select the point of insertion.*
Select parts to write out.
Select objects: *Select the part or parts to export.*

ADPARTOUT TUTORIAL

This tutorial uses a multiple-part drawing and exports one of the parts to a separate file.

1. Open the part1 drawing you created in Chapter 13.

    Command: **open**

Open part1.dwg by selecting the drive and the directory of the file and then selecting the file.
Choose **OK.**

2. Use the ADPARTOUT command to export the ball from the drawing.

Command: **adpartout**

Enter file name: **ball.dwg**

Select insert point: *Select anywhere on the ball.*

Select parts to write out.

Select objects: *Select the ball.*

ADPARTIN

ADPARTIN imports previously created AutoCAD Designer parts with the .dwg extension into the current AutoCAD Designer drawing. A part that has been imported using ADPARTIN is fully editable and is in no way linked to the original part. One use of ADPARTIN is to create an assembly drawing made up of AutoCAD Designer parts. This command is very similar to the AutoCAD INSERT command, except that ADPARTIN inserts only AutoCAD Designer data.

Helpful Hint: It is not recommended to use the AutoCAD INSERT command to import AutoCAD Designer parts.

Command: **adpartin**

Enter file name: *Enter the file name.*

Select insert point: *Select a location where the part or parts will be placed.*

ADPARTIN TUTORIAL

This tutorial shows how to use the ADPARTIN command to insert previously created models into a current drawing.

1. Open the extrude1 drawing you created in Chapter 4.

Command: **open**

Open extrude1.dwg by selecting the drive and the directory of the file and then selecting the file.
Choose **OK.**

2. Use the ADPARTIN command to import the ball into the drawing.

Command: **adpartin**

Enter file name: **ball.dwg**

Select insert point: *Select anywhere near the block.*

Your new multiple-part drawing should be similar to Figure 15–1.

ADSATOUT

ADSATOUT creates a standard ACIS file with the .sat extension from an AutoCAD Designer part. Through the use of .sat files, 3D data can be transferred between systems.

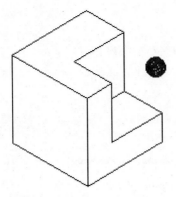

Figure 15-1

Command: **adsatout**
File name: *Enter a name for the file.*

ADSATOUT TUTORIAL

In this tutorial you create a .sat file and then confirm that the file has in fact been created.

1. Open the chain link you created in Chapter 6.

    Command: **open**
    Open sweep1.dwg by selecting the drive and the directory of the file and then selecting the file.
    Choose **OK.**

2. Use the ADSATOUT command to export the drawing as a .sat file.
    Command: **adsatout**
    File name: **transfer1** ↵

3. Check your File Manager to see that the file was created.

ADSATIN

ADSATIN imports a standard ACIS file with the .sat extension into AutoCAD Designer. During the translating process, ACIS solid bodies are converted and assigned an AutoCAD Designer part ID. These bodies may then be used as base features. Wire bodies are not converted during the .sat import process.

Command: **adsatin**
Enter a .sat file name (including extension): *Enter the file name.*

ADASFCONV

ADASFCONV translates AutoCAD Designer parts into a collection of AutoSurf surfaces. How the AutoCAD Designer parts are translated depends on the settings of the surface conversion variables. AutoSurf does not have to be loaded to use the ADASFCONV command.

Command: **adasfconv**

Select parts to convert.

Select objects: *Select the part or parts for conversion.*

The Surface Conversion Variables dialogue box is shown in Figure 15–2.

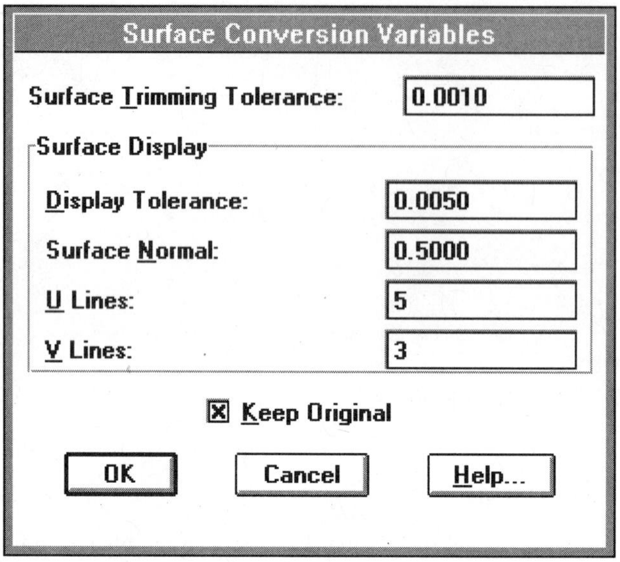

Figure 15-2

Surface Trimming Tolerance   The Surface Trimming Tolerance controls the value that is used when ADASFCONV chords the NURBS curves into polylines from the AutoCAD Designer part. These polylines are used as the borders for trimming the AutoSurf surfaces. The default value is 0.001 when AutoSurf is not loaded; however, if AutoSurf is loaded, this value defaults to the current value of the AutoSurf system variable ASSYSTOL.

Surface Display

Display Tolerance   Sets the tolerance used for display lines for the AutoSurf surfaces, which are created using ADASFCONV. When AutoSurf is loaded, the default value is the current value of the AutoSurf system variable ASSURFDISP. When AutoSurf is not loaded, the default value is 0.005.

Surface Normal   Sets the length of the normal vector shown within the AutoSurf surface display. When AutoSurf is loaded, the default value is the current setting of the AutoSurf system variable ASSURFVECTOR; the value is 0.5 when AutoSurf is not loaded.

U Lines   Sets the number of lines shown in the U direction of the AutoSurf surfaces when created by ADASFCONV. When AutoSurf is loaded, the default value is the current setting of the AutoSurf system variable ASSURFU; the value is 5 when AutoSurf is not loaded.

V Lines   Sets the number of lines shown in the V direction of the AutoSurf surfaces when created by ADASFCONV. When AutoSurf is loaded, the default value is the current setting of the AutoSurf system variable ASSURFV; the value is 3 when AutoSurf is not loaded.

Keep Original   Toggles between whether or not the AutoCAD Designer part or parts will be deleted after they are converted using the ADASFCONV command. The default setting, a checked box, prevents the AutoCAD Designer parts from being deleted after they are converted.

ADASFCONV TUTORIAL

In this tutorial you will create a surface drawing used for AutoSurf.

1. Open the chain link you created in Chapter 6.

   Command: **open**

   Open sweep1.dwg by selecting the drive and the directory of the file and then selecting the file.

   Choose **OK.**

2. Use the ADASFCONV command to translate the drawing into surfaces.

   Command: **adasfconv**

   Select parts to convert.

   Select objects: *Pick the link.*

   File name: **transfer1**

   Keep the default settings in the dialogue box in Figure 15–3 as shown and select OK.

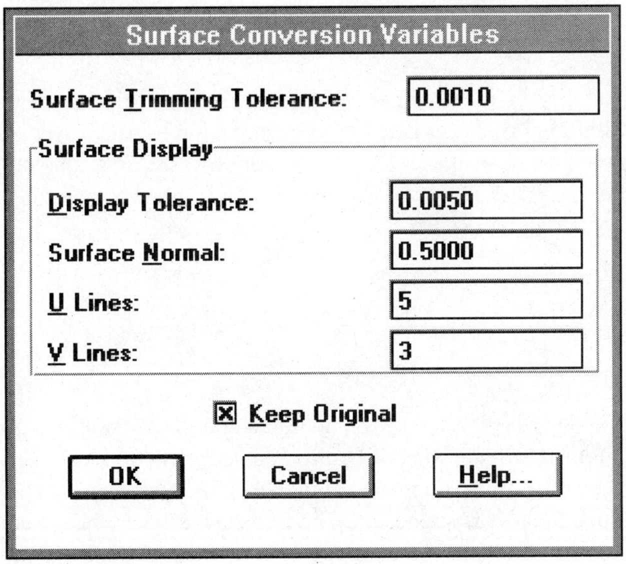

Surface Conversion Variables

Surface **T**rimming Tolerance:	0.0010

Surface Display

Display Tolerance:	0.0050
Surface **N**ormal:	0.5000
U Lines:	5
V Lines:	3

[X] **K**eep Original

[OK]   [Cancel]   [**H**elp...]

Figure 15-3

REVIEW QUESTIONS

15.1 Give an example of how to use the ADPARTOUT command.

15.2 Give an example of how to use the ADPARTIN command.

15.3 Which command is used when you want to create a StereoLithography file for rapid prototyping?

15.4 What type of files are imported with the ADSATIN command?

15.5 What does the ADASFCONV command do?

15.6 Briefly explain each of the options that need to be set with the ADASFCONV command.

CHAPTER EXERCISES

15.1 Use the ADPARTIN command to create a multiple-part drawing with any models you created in previous exercises.

appendix

A

AUTOCAD HINTS

Understanding AutoCAD will enhance your ability to fully utilize the tools and capabilities of AutoCAD Designer. However, a simple knowledge of some basic drafting principles and a brief introduction to AutoCAD are all you need to be able to understand the three-dimensional parametric-based AutoCAD Designer program. This appendix presents some simple AutoCAD tips that can help you use AutoCAD Designer more efficiently. We assume that you are familiar with AutoCAD's basic commands, such as LINE, ARC, and CIRCLE.

LAYERS

It is good practice within AutoCAD Designer to set up separate layers for sketching, dimensioning, construction lines, and the solid model. The recommended basic four layers are Model, Dimension, Construction, and Scrap.

Your Model layer should include only your actual three-dimensional model. This layer needs to be of a continuous linetype. Any color is acceptable, although blue, color 4, is suggested. The Dimension layer should contain all dimensions made through AutoCAD dimensioning options, AutoCAD Designer parametric dimensioning options, or reference dimensioning options. This layer also needs to be of a continuous linetype, and red, color 1, is recommended.

The next layer, Construction, should include any construction lines or points that will be used for your reference or for AutoCAD Designer dimensioning reference. The Construction layer needs to be a linetype other than continuous in order for AutoCAD Designer to treat the objects on this layer as construction objects. A linetype of hidden or phantom is recommended along with color 2, yellow. The last layer needed for AutoCAD Designer is the Scrap layer on which you will draw any sketch geometry that is used for paths or profiles. For this layer, we recommend a continuous linetype and green, color 3, for a bright contrast. You will be using these paths and profiles to add new features to your model. They are the focus of attention and need to stand out from the model.

We highly recommend that you add these layers to your drawing, for they are referenced throughout the tutorial sections of this book. Variances of the above layers may be used and additional layers may be added as necessary. You can save time by creating these layers and saving them in a prototype drawing file and using it at the beginning of each new drawing file.

The following section describes the procedure for creating layers. We suggest that you practice this procedure now so that you are familiar with it when you begin the tutorials. First you need to access the Layer Control dialogue box by selecting the layer control option, which is a submenu of the Settings pull-down menu, or by clicking on the layer icon

 with your mouse. The Layer Control dialogue box is shown in Figure A–1.

In the name box, above the OK button at the bottom of the window, type **MODEL**, then select New. This layer should have been added to the bottom of the list of layers that are currently in your drawing. Highlight the new Model layer with your mouse and select Set Color, pick Blue, #4, and OK. If the linetype is not already set to continuous, change it by selecting Set Ltype and then selecting Continuous. Follow this procedure for setting the Dimension, Construction, and Scrap layers as well.

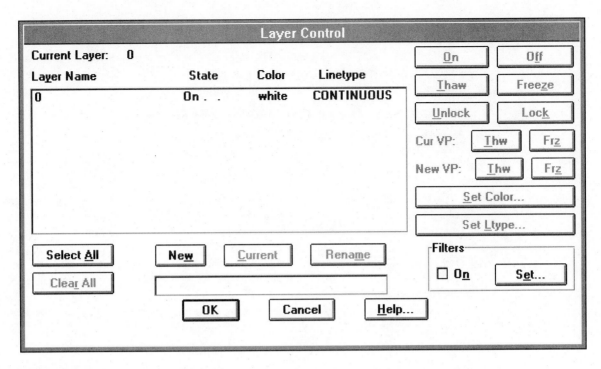

Figure A-1

Note: You might need to load the hidden or phantom linetype for your Construction layer if it is not already loaded. To do this type **linetype** at the command prompt. Select **l** for load and type **hidden, phantom**. Accept the default file from which to load the linetypes.

When you are finished creating your layers, your Layer Control dialogue box should appear as shown in Figure A–2.

Note: Your layers might be shown in a different order.

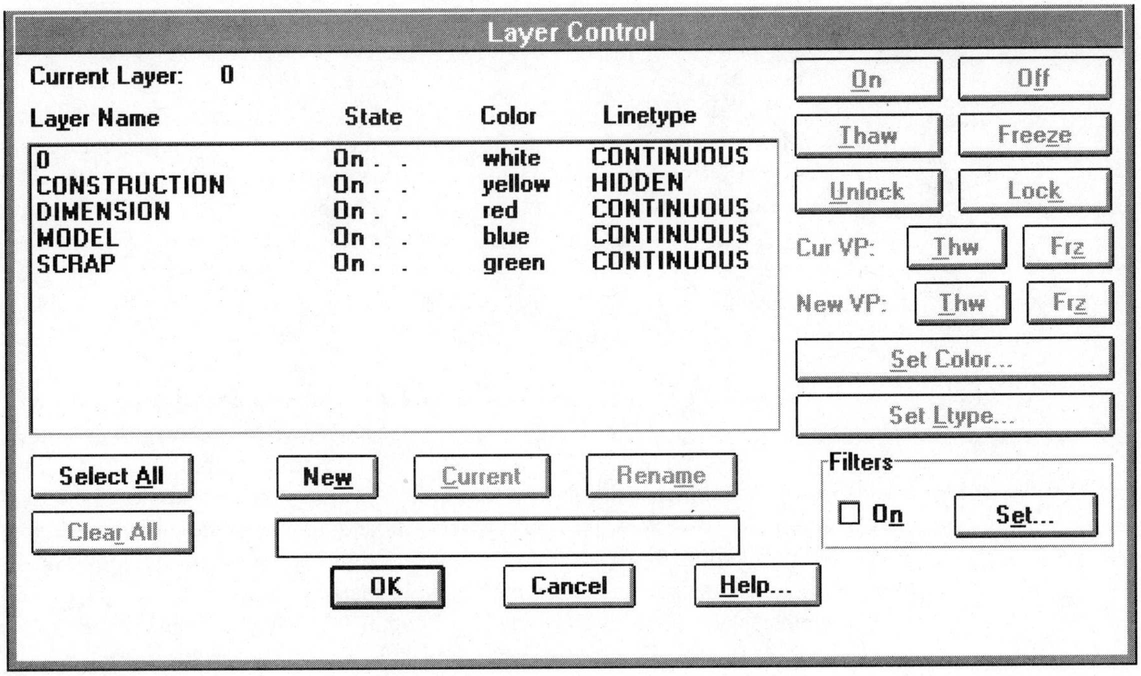

Figure A-2

In addition to the four layers that you have just created, AutoCAD Designer creates seven layers of its own. They are ADD_DIMS, ADD_VIEWS, ADP_WORK, ADP_FRZ, ADV_#_HID, ADV_#_VIS, and ADV_#_SEC. The first four are created automatically when the AutoCAD Designer program is loaded. AutoCAD Designer organizes different sections of your drawing on these layers as follows:

ADD_DIMS   Contains the parametric dimensions you create.

ADD_VIEW   Contains the viewport borders.

ADP_WORK   Contains work plane, work axis, and work-point geometry.

ADP_FRZ   Contains any frozen parametric dimensions in the drawing views.

AutoCAD Designer creates the ADV_VIS and ADV_HID layers each time you add a two-dimensional drawing view to your database. ADV_SEC layers are created only if you make a section view. The # symbol corresponds to the view number that you just created. Therefore, your drawing may have many ADV_VIS layers, each one representing a different two-dimensional view. AutoCAD Designer places the visible-part geometry on the ADV_VIS layers, the hidden-part geometry on the ADV_HID layers, and section lines on the ADV_SEC layers.

Note: Never work on any of these layers!! Altering their contents may permanently corrupt your database!!

UNDO-Mark/Back

When you begin working with AutoCAD Designer, the basic commands may seem fairly simple. However, as the complexity of your drawings increases and the number of dimensions and constraints in a profile grows, you will find that setting marked points throughout your drawing can save you a lot of time when you make a mistake. Not that you will make any mistakes your first time around, but it is good practice to use these commands just in case.

When creating a model, it is easy to make a mistake and continue with several steps before realizing that you need to return to make a correction. In addition, one command sometimes completes several steps. Thus you cannot use the AutoCAD U command because the U command simply undoes the last command entered. However, AutoCAD's UNDO Mark and UNDO Back commands allow you to undo steps in increments that you specifically marked.

Use the UNDO Mark command after you have accomplished a step in building your model or have reached a point that you do not want to lose accidentally. At the command prompt, type **UNDO**. Since you wish to mark this point, type **M** at the prompt. Anytime that you want to return to this point, use the UNDO Back command. UNDO Back returns you to the last UNDO mark. A second UNDO Back returns you to an earlier mark. Once an UNDO Back command is used, the marked point it returns to is removed. You must remark the point if you want to use it again! You can mark as many points as you like. Marking the simplest of accomplishments is recommended, especially with the complexity of AutoCAD Designer.

For example, while you are parametrically dimensioning a profile, you may continue to add dimensions one after another but use the ADPARDIM command only once. This technique can get you into some trouble when you wish to back up. If you try UNDO after entering the last dimension, you will lose every dimension you created after the ADPARDIM command. Therefore, it is good practice to add a mark in the middle of dimensioning your profile or path, especially in complex designs. If you do need to go back, simply use the UNDO Back command to return to your marked point.

Another place where the UNDO Mark command is helpful is just before executing one of the AutoCAD Designer feature commands. Rather than editing features after you realize that your feature needs to be changed, you can simply return to your marked point to modify any dimensions. This is especially useful when you are experimenting with a drawing and you know that you will have to come back and change dimensions.

Since the tutorials are fairly simple, the UNDO-Mark/Back commands are not used between dimensioning steps; however, some of the tutorials use the commands prior to executing a feature as a reminder to you of their existence. Start using these commands regularly as you learn AutoCAD Designer. If you wait until you actually get into some complex drawings, you may forget to use the commands and miss out on their time saving benefits.

VIEWPORTS

AutoCAD's VPORTS command allows you to split your screen to see multiple views of a model at the same time. A prime example of this is setting the left half of the screen to view your part based on the current active sketch plane and setting the right half of the screen to view the part from an isometric point of view. Your screen might look similar to Figure A–3.

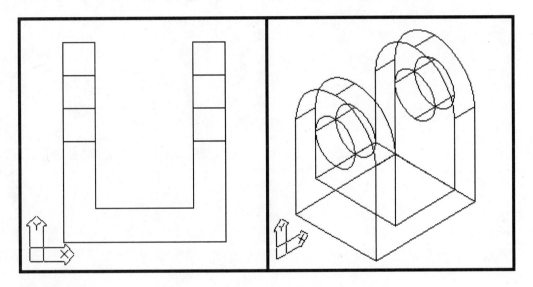

Figure A-3

To make a viewport active, simply click inside it. This method simplifies dimensioning by allowing you to select objects in the viewport where it is most convenient. To set your screen this way, follow the steps below.

1. Activate the AutoCAD VPORTS command and create two vertical viewports.

    Command: **vports**

    Save/Restore/Delete/Join/SIngle/?/2/<3>/4: **2**

    Horizontal/<Vertical>: **vertical**

2. Make the left viewport active by clicking inside it and set the AutoCAD UCSFOLLOW system variable to 1, which allows the view to change according to the current UCS.

    Command: **ucsfollow**

    New value for UCSFOLLOW<0>: **1**

3. It is also advised that you make the right viewport active and perform a ZOOM, EXTENTS to make the current view the size of the current viewport.

For further information about AutoCAD's VPORTS command, refer to your AutoCAD manual.

TRANSPARENT COMMANDS

Some AutoCAD commands can be performed transparently within other AutoCAD commands. The first of these commands is ZOOM. While running another command, you might find that in order to select the needed entity you need to perform a ZOOM. Type in **'Z** or **'ZOOM** on the command line instead of the expected input. You will be allowed to zoom to select the needed entity, and then your previous command will resume where it left off. Other commands that work this way are PAN and DDLMODES. Again, to utilize these commands transparently, simply precede them with an apostrophe ('). AutoCAD's PAN shifts the current screen image to a distance specified by either a numerical value or a crosshair displacement. DDLMODES engages AutoCAD's Layer dialogue box, which allows you to turn on or off selected layers in order to choose a specific entity that may lie too close to an entity on a different layer. These are extremely useful commands once you learn how to use them. Incorporate them into your modeling to familiarize yourself with their usage. Unfortunately, these transparent commands work only in Model space (Part mode).

PULL-DOWN MENUS

MAIN MENU

Designer	
Sketch ▶	Sketch Submenu
Features ▶	Features Submenu
Drawing ▶	Drawing Submenu
Edit Feature	ADEDITFEAT
Change Dimension	ADMODDIM
Update	ADUPDATE
Part ▶	Part Submenu
Mode	ADMODE
Part Viewing ▶	Part Viewing Submenu
Display ▶	Display Submenu
Parameters ▶	Parameters Submenu
Utilities ▶	Utilities Submenu
Settings...	ADSETTINGS
About Designer...	ADVER
Designer Help...	HELP
Search for Help on...	
How to Use Help...	

SKETCH SUBMENU

Profile	ADPROFILE
Path	ADPATH
Sketch Plane	ADSKPLN
Constraints ▶	Constraints Submenu
Fix Point	ADFIXPT
Add Dimension	ADPARDIM

SKETCH/CONSTRAINTS SUBMENU

Show	ADSHOWCON
Add	ADADDCON
Delete	ADDELCON

FEATURES SUBMENU

Extrude...	ADEXTRUDE
Revolve...	ADREVOLVE
Sweep	ADSWEEP
Hole...	ADHOLE
Fillet	ADFILLET
Chamfer...	ADCHAMFER
Work Plane...	ADWORKPLN
Work Axis	ADWORKAXIS
Work Point	ADWORKPT
Delete	ADDELFEAT

DRAWING SUBMENU

Create View...	ADVIEW
Edit View ▶	Drawing/Edit View Submenu
Dimension ▶	Drawing/Dimension Submenu
Annotation ▶	Drawing/Annotations Submenu

DRAWING/EDIT VIEW SUBMENU

Attributes	ADEDITVIEW
Delete	ADDELVIEW
Move	ADMOVEVIEW

DRAWING/DIMENSION SUBMENU

Ref Dim	ADREFDIM
Delete Ref Dim	ADDELREF
Move	ADMOVEDIM
Freeze	ADFRZDIM
Thaw	ADTHAWDIM
Attributes	ADDIMATT

DRAWING/ANNOTATION SUBMENU

Create	ADANNOTE, Create
Delete	ADANNOTE, Delete
Move	ADANNOTE, Move
Add	ADANNOTE, Add
Remove	ADANNOTE, Remove
Move Leader	ADMOVELDR
Hole Note	ADHOLENOTE

PART SUBMENU

New	ADNEWPART
Make Active	ADACTPART

PART VIEWING SUBMENU

Front	ADPARTVIEW, Front
Right	ADPARTVIEW, Right
Left	ADPARTVIEW, Left
Top	ADPARTVIEW, Top
Bottom	ADPARTVIEW, Bottom
Iso	ADPARTVIEW, Iso
Sketch	ADPARTVIEW, Sketch

DISPLAY SUBMENU

Mesh ▶	Display/Mesh Submenu
Isolines	ADISOLINES
Dim Display	ADDIMDSP
Work Plane ▶	Display/Work Plane Submenu
Work Axis ▶	Display/Work Axis Submenu
Work Point ▶	Display/Work Point Submenu

DRAWING/MESH SUBMENU

On	ADMESH, On
Off	ADMESH, Off

DRAWING/WORK PLANE SUBMENU

On	ADWORKPLN, On
Off	ADWORKPLN, Off

DRAWING/WORK AXIS SUBMENU

On	ADWORKAXIS, On
Off	ADWORKAXIS, Off

DRAWING/WORK POINT SUBMENU

On	ADWORKPT, On
Off	ADWORKPT, Off

PARAMETERS SUBMENU

Create	ADPARAM, Create
Delete	ADPARAM, Delete
List	ADPARAM, List
Import...	ADPARAM, Import
Export...	ADPARAM, Export
Linked File	ADPARFILE

UTILITIES SUBMENU

Make Base	ADMAKEBASE
List ▶	Utilities/List Submenu
Mass Properties	ADMASSPROP
Transfer ▶	Utilities/Transfer Submenu
Show Active	ADSHOWACT
Toolbars ▶	Utilities/Toolbars Submenu
Load Designer	Load Designer
Unload Designer	Unlaod Designer

UTILITIES/LIST SUBMENU

Part	ADLIST, Part
Feature	ADLIST, Feature
Drawing View	ADLIST, View

UTILITIES/TRANSFER SUBMENU

Part Out...	ADPARTOUT
Part In...	ADPARTIN
SAT Out...	ADSATOUT
SAT In...	ADSATIN
AutoSurf Out	ADAFSCONV

UTILITIES/TOOLBARS SUBMENU

Designer Main	Show Designer Main Toolbar
Designer View	Show Designer View Toolbar

GLOSSARY

ADACTPART Switches the active part of a multiple-part drawing.

ADADDCON Places relationships between the part geometry of the active sketch.

ADANNOTE Creates annotations that are parametrically bound to the drawing views.

ADASFCONV Translates AutoCAD Designer models into a collection of AutoSurf surfaces.

ADAXISDSP Toggles the display of the work axes.

ADCHAMFER Places a chamfer along a selected edge or edges of the active part.

ADDELCON Deletes any existing constraints from the active sketch.

ADDELFEAT Removes a selected feature from the active part.

ADDELREF Deletes selected reference dimensions from the orthographic views.

ADDELVIEW Removes a specified drawing view.

ADDIMATT Changes the properties of the drawing view dimensions.

ADDIMDSP Changes the dimension display between numeric, parameters, or equations.

ADEDITFEAT Modifies a selected feature of the active part.

ADEDITVIEW Modifies the scale, associated text, and line display of the selected drawing view.

ADEXTRUDE Projects a profile into the z-axis for the creation of a solid object. Used to construct features of a model.

ADFILLET Creates a radius along a selected edge or edges of the active part.

ADFIXPT Makes one point of the active sketch fixed on its position in the XYZ coordinate system relative to the remaining sketch entities.

ADFRZDIM Freezes selected dimensions from the orthographic views.

ADHOLE Creates drilled holes, counterbores, and countersinks in the active part.

ADHOLENOTE Automates the creation of a leader with the diameter depth and angle information listed for a selected hole in the drawing.

ADISOLINES Controls the display of curved faces during a wire-frame representation.

ADLIST Provides information about the features, parts, and views in the drawing.

ADMAKEBASE Creates a static, uneditable, compressed part.

ADMASSPROP Calculates and displays the three-dimensional properties of the model including volume, mass, and center of gravity.

ADMESH Toggles the display of the model between a wire-frame representation and a mesh representation.

ADMODDIM Changes parametric dimension values on the active sketch or on the drawing.

ADMODE Toggles between Part mode and Drawing mode.

ADMOVEDIM Moves dimensions in the AutoCAD Designer Orthographic views while maintaining their association to the part's geometry.

ADMOVELDR Relocates the start point of an annotation leader.

ADMOVEVIEW Repositions views anywhere on the drawing as long as they stay within the restrictions of their view type.

ADNEWPART Begins a new part of a multiple-part drawing.

ADPARAM Creates, deletes, lists, exports, and imports global parameters used for dimensioning.

ADPARDIM Creates dimension entities that control the active sketch parametrically.

ADPARTIN Imports previously created AutoCAD Designer parts of the .dwg extension into the current AutoCAD Designer drawing.

ADPARTOUT Writes AutoCAD Designer parts into separate .dwg files.

ADPARTVIEW Lets the model be viewed from various orientations.

ADPATH Creates an active path for the sweep feature from the selected geometry.

ADPLNDSP Toggles the display of work planes.

ADPROFILE Creates an active sketch from selected geometry.

ADPTDSP Toggles the display of work points.

ADREFDIM Creates reference dimensions on the orthographic views.

ADREVOLVE Uses an axis of rotation to revolve a profile around for the construction of a solid feature.

ADSATIN Imports a standard ACIS file with the .sat extension into AutoCAD Designer.

ADSATOUT Creates a standard ACIS file with the .sat extension from an AutoCAD Designer part.

ADSETTINGS Changes the AutoCAD Designer system variables.

ADSHOWACT Highlights the active part, sketch, or sketch plane.

ADSHOWCON Displays the existing constraints on the active sketch.

ADSKPLN Sets the current location of the sketch plane along with the XY orientation.

ADSWEEP Creates a solid three-dimensional feature by taking a two-dimensional sketch and sweeping it along a user-defined path.

ADTHAWDIM Thaws frozen dimensions from the orthographic views.

ADUPDATE Regenerates the active part and drawing and incorporates modifications.

ADVER Displays the version number of the AutoCAD Designer software.

ADVIEW Creates two-dimensional as well as isometric views in Paper space.

ADWORKAXIS Creates a work axis that is automatically constrained to pass through the center line of a cylindrical, conical, or toroidal surface.

ADWORKPLN Creates an infinite plane in space; used to define sketch planes, define feature placements and terminations, and define section planes.

ADWORKPT Creates work points for the construction of hole features.

A

Active Part Model currently recognized by AutoCAD Designer commands.

Active Profile Profile currently recognized by AutoCAD Designer commands.

Active Sketch Plane Current sketch plane where two-dimensional geometry is created.

B

Base Feature The first three-dimensional feature created for a part.

C

Chamfer One of the six fundamental features.

Child Dependency A feature or orthographic view that is dependent on a previously created feature or view.

Collinear Constraint Relates two different lines by making them in line with each other.

Concentric Constraint Confines two circles or arcs to have the same center point.

Constraint A geometric definition given to an entity.

D

Dimension A numeric constraint consisting of a length, radius, diameter, or angle.

Draft Angle The angle of tapering, either positive or negative, applied to a feature.

Drawing Mode Where all two-dimensional drawing views in AutoCAD Designer are created. Also known as Paper Space.

E

Entity A line or arc segment of a sketch.

Extrusion One of the six fundamental features.

F

Feature A three-dimensional entity created by a profile that has either been extruded, revolved, or swept along a path. Features can also be holes, fillets, or chamfers.

Fillet One of the six fundamental features.

Fully Constrained Sketch A sketch that requires no interpretations by AutoCAD Designer.

G

Global Parameters Dimensional equations such as Length = 5.

H

Hole One of the six fundamental features.

Horizontal Constraint Confines a line segment to be parallel with the x-axis.

I

Isolines Lines displayed on the surface of a part for visual aid.

J

Join Constraint Closes the gap between the endpoints of two entities.

M

Model Also referred to as a part.

Model Space See Part mode.

N

Negative Draft Angle Draft angle that tapers inward or narrows the feature.

Normal Perpendicular to each other.

NURBS Nonuniform rational B splines.

P

Paper Space See Drawing mode.

Parallel Having the same slope.

Parallel Constraint Confines two lines to have the same slope.

Parameter A variable defined by the user to dimension a part.

Parent View A feature or orthographic view that has child dependencies.

Part See model.

Part Mode Where all models in AutoCAD Designer are created. Also known as Model space.

Perpendicular Constraint Confines two lines to lie 90 degrees apart from each other.

Polylines A series of connected lines.

Positive Draft Angle Draft angle that tapers outward or widens the feature.

Profile Geometry defining the two-dimensional cross-section of a feature.

Projected Constraint Confines the endpoint of an entity onto a line.

R

Radius Constraint Confines two circles or arcs to have the same radius.

Revolution One of the six fundamental features.

S

Sketch Geometry created on the sketch plane that is used to create a profile or path.

Sketch Plane An infinite plane in space on which the next path or profile will be sketched.

Sweep One of the six fundamental features.

System Variables Control the rules that AutoCAD Designer follows when interpreting your sketch. Set by the ADSETTINGS command.

T

Tangent Constraint Confines two objects to have the same slope at their intersection point.

U

UCS See user coordinate system.

User Coordinate System Determines the orientation for two-dimensional objects.

V

Vertical Constraint Confines a line segment to be parallel with the y-axis.

W

WCS See world coordinate system

Work Axis A reference line created through a cylinder used for locating a sketch or work plane; can also be used as an axis of revolution for revolving a profile around.

Work Plane   A defined plane in space used as a sketch plane, reference for dimensioning a sketch, or cutting plane for defining cross-sections in drawing views.

Work Point   A defined point in space used to locate a hole.

World Coordinate System   The default UCS orientation.

X-Y

XValue Constraint   Confines two circles or arcs to have the same X coordinate center point.

Yvalue Constraint   Confines two circles or arcs to have the same Y coordinate center point.

Index